D1546732

Linux for Developers

Developer's Library

Linux
for Developers
Jumpstart your Linux Programming Skills

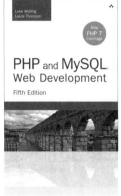

PHP and MySQL
Web Development
Fifth Edition

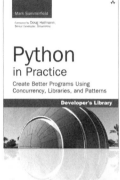

Python
in Practice
Create Better Programs Using
Concurrency, Libraries, and Patterns

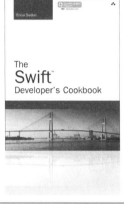

The
Swift™
Developer's Cookbook

Visit **informit.com/devlibrary** for a complete list of available publications.

The **Developer's Library** series from Addison-Wesley provides practicing programmers with unique, high-quality references and tutorials on the latest programming languages and technologies they use in their daily work. All books in the Developer's Library are written by expert technology practioners who are exceptionally skilled at organizing and presenting information in a way that is useful for other programmers.

Developer's Library titles cover a wide range of topics, from open source programming languages and technologies, mobile application development, and web development to Java programming and more.

Pearson

the trusted technology learning source

✦ Addison-Wesley

Linux for Developers

Jumpstart Your Linux Programming Skills

William "Bo" Rothwell

✦✦Addison-Wesley

Boston • Columbus • Indianapolis • New York • San Francisco • Amsterdam
Cape Town Dubai • London • Madrid • Milan • Munich • Paris • Montreal
Toronto • Delhi • Mexico City Sao Paulo • Sidney • Hong Kong • Seoul
Singapore • Taipei • Tokyo

Many of the designations used by manufacturers and sellers to distinguish their products are claimed as trademarks. Where those designations appear in this book, and the publisher was aware of a trademark claim, the designations have been printed with initial capital letters or in all capitals.

The author and publisher have taken care in the preparation of this book, but make no expressed or implied warranty of any kind and assume no responsibility for errors or omissions. No liability is assumed for incidental or consequential damages in connection with or arising out of the use of the information or programs contained herein.

For information about buying this title in bulk quantities, or for special sales opportunities (which may include electronic versions; custom cover designs; and content particular to your business, training goals, marketing focus, or branding interests), please contact our corporate sales department at corpsales@pearsoned.com or (800) 382-3419.

For government sales inquiries, please contact governmentsales@pearsoned.com.

For questions about sales outside the U.S., please contact intlcs@pearsoned.com.

Visit us on the Web: informit.com/aw

Library of Congress Control Number: 2017932512

Copyright © 2017 Pearson Education, Inc.

All rights reserved. Printed in the United States of America. This publication is protected by copyright, and permission must be obtained from the publisher prior to any prohibited reproduction, storage in a retrieval system, or transmission in any form or by any means, electronic, mechanical, photocopying, recording, or likewise. For information regarding permissions, request forms and the appropriate contacts within the Pearson Education Global Rights & Permissions Department, please visit www.pearsoned.com/permissions/.

ISBN-13: 978-0-13-465728-8

ISBN-10: 0-13-465728-4

1   17

Editor-in-Chief
Mark Taub

Executive Editor
Debra Williams Cauley

Development Editor
Chris Zahn

Managing Editor
Sandra Schroeder

Senior Project Editor
Lori Lyons

Project Manager
Dhayanidhi

Copy Editor
Paula Lowell

Indexer
Cheryl Lenser

Proofreader
SathishKumar

Technical Reviewers
Matthew Helmke
Keith Wright

Editorial Assistant
Kim Boedigheimer

Cover Designer
Chuti Prasertsith

Compositor
codeMantra

❖

"A best friend is the only one that walks into your life when the world has walked out."
— Shannon L. Alder

Thank you, Sarah, my love and my wife, for walking into my life.

"Strong people don't put others down... They lift them up."
— Michael P. Watson

Thank you, Mom and Dad, for being supportive.

"Fall seven times, stand up eight."
— Japanese Proverb

Thank you, Julia, for being understanding.

❖

Contents at a Glance

Contents

Preface

When I envisioned this book, I thought of it as the beginning of a journey. Your exact starting point on this journey may differ from that of others, but the purpose of this book is to provide you with what you need to know to start developing software on a Linux Operating System.

Some readers will already have software developing experience on Windows-based platforms. For those folks, this book should serve as a guide to how software development differs on Linux from the platform you are used to developing on.

Perhaps you already work in Linux, but want to start writing code. Again, this book will provide you with an excellent starting point for that journey.

The book is organized into four parts.

- Part I, "Open Source Software," contains a single chapter—Chapter 1, "Introduction to Open Source Software." You learn about open source software, including its advantages over closed source software, as well as some essentials regarding software licenses.

- In Part II, "Linux Essentials," you are introduced to the Linux operating system. The goal of this part is to provide you with the key knowledge that software developers need to know while working in Linux. This includes both end user and administration topics. The chapters in this part include the following:

  - Chapter 2, "Introduction to Linux." In this chapter you learn the basics of Linux, including how to access a Linux system, how to use a Linux-based GUI, and basic command-line execution.

  - Chapter 3, "The Filesystem." This chapter focuses on how the files are organized in Linux. You are introduced to filesystem concepts, learn how to navigate the filesystem, and learn how to manage the filesystem.

  - Chapter 4, "Essential Commands." In this chapter you learn a variety of Linux commands that are critical for any developer to know.

  - Chapter 5, "Text Editors." As a developer, you need to know how to edit files. This chapter focuses on the vi editor, a common text editor in both Linux and Unix. You are also introduced to additional Linux editors.

  - Chapter 6, "System Administration." It is helpful to know how to perform system administration tasks, even as a developer. You learn how to add software and administer users in this chapter.

- Part III, "Linux Programming Languages," provides an overview of different programming languages available in Linux. You have a lot of choices here! The goal here isn't to teach you everything about each language but to introduce you to many of them so you can decide which language will work best for you.

  - Chapter 7, "Overview of Programming Languages." This chapter provides an overview of programming languages with the focus on distinguishing between scripting languages and structured (or compiled) languages.

- Chapter 8, "BASH Shell Scripting." In this chapter you are introduced to the BASH shell language. You learn how to create code that interacts with users as well as other features of the BASH shell programming language.

- Chapter 9, "Perl Scripting." The focus of this chapter is how to program in the Perl scripting language. Topics include flow control and variable usage.

- Chapter 10, "Python Scripting." You learn the basics of Python scripting in this chapter, including the large variety of Python variable types, and how to reuse code and flow control.

- Chapter 11, "C, C++, and Java." In this chapter you learn the essentials to create C, C++, and Java code on Linux-based systems.

- Lastly, Part IV, "Using GIT," covers a very popular software revision control product called Git. Using a revision control product, especially when working with teams of developers, can save a lot of time, money, and effort.

  - Chapter 12, "GIT Essentials." In this chapter you learn the concepts of GIT. Topics include revision control concepts, GIT installation, and GIT features.

  - Chapter 13, "Manage Files with GIT." In this chapter you learn how to use GIT features such as staging, committing, and branches.

  - Chapter 14, "Manage Differences in Files." The focus of this chapter is on how to deal with different versions of files. You learn how to execute diffs (differences in files) and merge files.

  - Chapter 15, "Advanced GIT Features." You learn how to manage GIT repositories and perform patching in this chapter.

Good luck in your journey!

—William "Bo" Rothwell
December 22, 2016

Register your copy of *Linux for Developers* at informit.com for convenient access to downloads, updates, and corrections as they become available. To start the registration process, go to informit.com/register and log in or create an account. Enter the product ISBN 9780134657288 and click Submit. Once the process is complete, you will find any available bonus content under "Registered Products".

Acknowledgments

Thanks to all who helped me put this book together. As any decent author will tell you, there are many, many hours put into a publication like this, which were the results of other people's efforts and dedication.

Keith Wright and Matthew Helmke, thank your technical reviews. There is no doubt this is a much better book than my original effort because of your feedback.

Chris Zahn: I couldn't have asked for a better editor. You make me look like I can put together a coherent sentence—no small feat!

Debra Williams Cauley, thanks for seeing the value and providing a guiding hand throughout this process.

About the Author

At the impressionable age of 14, **William "Bo" Rothwell** crossed paths with a TRS-80 Micro Computer System (affectionately known as a "Trash 80"). Soon after, the adults responsible for Bo made the mistake of leaving him alone with the TSR-80. He immediately dismantled it and held his first computer class, showing his friends what made this "computer thing" work.

Since this experience, Bo's passion for understanding how computers work and sharing this knowledge with others has resulted in a rewarding career in IT training. His experience includes Linux, Unix, and programming languages such as Perl, Python, Tcl, and BASH. He is the founder and lead instructor of One Course Source, an IT training organization.

Open Source Software

One of the most important questions you need to answer when creating software is, "Under what type of license will this software be released?" Arriving at that answer can be a difficult journey.

You must determine what sort of protection you want to place on your code as well as what you will allow others to do with the software that you create. This part includes just one chapter, focusing on helping you decide how to license your software. In this chapter, you learn the following:

- The difference between closed and open source software
- Open source protection concepts
- The difference between primary open source licenses

Introduction to Open Source Software

You have created an awesome program, and now you want to make it available to the public. Now comes an important decision to make: what license to apply to your software.

This decision will have several important impacts, including the following:

- How users can use your software
- Whether the code is visible to others or "hidden" from plain sight
- Whether other developers can use the code to create their own programs
- Whether others can sell (or resell) the program

Disclaimer

License issues can be complex and have a significant impact on how your software is used. The discussion in this book is designed to provide you with a basic understanding of different licenses but is not intended to provide any legal advice. The author of this book does not intend to provide any legal advice. Always consider consulting proper legal advice before making a decision regarding software licenses.

Defining Source Code

Most likely the first question you need to answer is, "Will this be closed source software or open source software?" To answer this question, you first need to understand what **source code** is.

Software consists of a collection of instructions that are written in a programming language. Dozens of different languages exist, including C, C++, Java, Perl, Python, and many others. This collection of instructions is referred to as source code. See Figure 1.1 for a demonstration of source code written in C.

```
/* Hello World program */

#include<stdio.h>

main()
{
     printf("Hello World");

}
```

Figure 1.1 Source code written in C

Typically, you can't use this source code directly to run your program. Most languages require a compile process in which the source code is converted into instructions that the operating system can understand. The result is data that looks like garbage to a human but makes sense to the operating system. See Figure 1.2 for a demonstration of source code that is converted into compiled code.

```
/* Hello World program */

#include<stdio.h>

main()
{
     printf("Hello World");

}
```

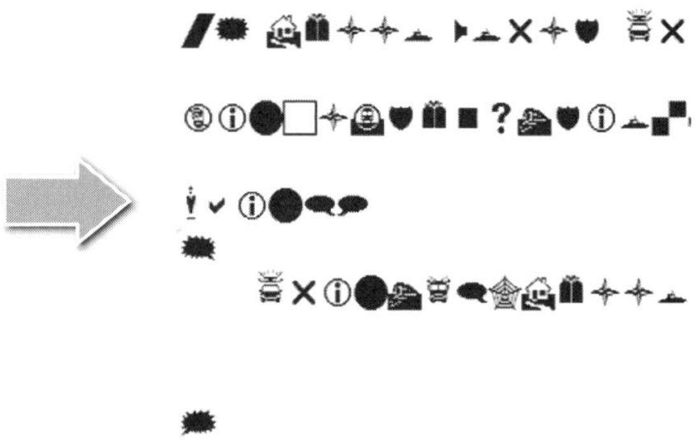

Figure 1.2 Example of source code converted to compiled code

If you choose to license your software as closed source, then you only provide the compiled code to customers. Software open source licenses include access to the original source code.

Closed Source

Also called **proprietary software**, the purpose of **closed source** software is to keep the source code a closely guarded secret. The idea is that if others can see the source code, then the source code may be copied and illegally used. As a result, competitors of the organization that created the software might end up having a negative impact on the financials of the organization that created the software. As you can imagine, copying someone else's software is much cheaper than creating your own software.

Often the term *closed source* is used in place of the term **commercial software**, but this isn't accurate. Commercial software must be purchased in order to use it. Both closed and open source software can be commercialized; the specific license determines whether the software is commercial or "free."[1]

Examples of closed source software include:

- Microsoft Windows
- Adobe Photoshop
- Apple macOS

Open Source

Software is considered open source when both the compiled and source versions of the code are made available.[2] The software license from the copyright holder grants certain rights to view, modify, and distribute the software. A variety of open source licenses are available that enable you to pick which rights are granted.

Although some open source software is free, in the economic sense, that isn't a requirement for open source software to be considered open source. Open source refers to the capability to access the source code, not how the software can be used or any costs associated with the software.

Common examples of open source software include:

- Linux[3]
- Apache HTTP Server
- Firefox
- Git
- Openoffice.org

"Free" Software

The concept of free in regards to software is not necessarily agreed upon by all. Some people might consider free software to be software without cost. In other words, it doesn't cost you anything to obtain and use the software.

---

1 There is a reason why I put *free* in quotes. As you will soon read, the term *free* must be legally defined in regards to software use.

2 Actually, some open source projects only provide the source code and leave it to the people who use the software to compile it. Additionally, some languages don't have a compile process, so a program written in such a language would only include the source code.

3 Technically, Linux refers to the Linux kernel, which is the heart of the Linux operating system. Most of the software found on Linux operating systems is also open source, but this isn't a requirement for inclusion in the OS.

However, what does it mean to use software? Does this mean that the software can be used in any way that the user wants, or are there some restrictions? Can this software be used anywhere in the world, or are there geographic limitations? Are you free to modify the software and distribute free copies of the modified format, or are these actions prohibited? As you can see, *free* in terms of software isn't so clear cut.

One way of defining the term *free* is to use the definition created by Richard Stallman and published by Free Software Foundation (FSF):

"The word 'free' in our name does not refer to price; it refers to freedom. First, the freedom to copy a program and redistribute it to your neighbors, so that they can use it as well as you. Second, the freedom to change a program, so that you can control it instead of it controlling you; for this, the source code must be made available to you."

Note that the preceding definition mandates that free software also be open source software. Not everyone agrees with this, and you will find some closed source freeware on the market.

Another way to define the term *free* is by the Four Freedoms, as defined by the Free Software Foundation:

- **Freedom 0:** "The freedom to run the program as you wish, for any purpose."

- **Freedom 1:** "The freedom to study how the program works and change it so it does your computing as you wish. Access to the source code is a precondition for this."

- **Freedom 2:** "The freedom to redistribute copies so you can help your neighbor."

- **Freedom 3:** "The freedom to distribute copies of your modified versions to others. By doing this you can give the whole community a chance to benefit from your changes. Access to the source code is a precondition for this."

These Four Freedoms are at the heart of what is referred to as **FOSS** (Free and Open Source Software).[4] FOSS attempts to address the challenge of defining what constitutes "free software." Note that the definition highlights the fact that not all free software is open source. Conversely, not all open source software is licensed with the Four Freedoms.

Understanding the complex world of open source software and what part "freedom" plays takes some time. See Figure 1.3 for a graphic that includes the various components of open source software.

---

4 Often used interchangeably with the term *FLOSS* (Free/Libre and Open Source Software).

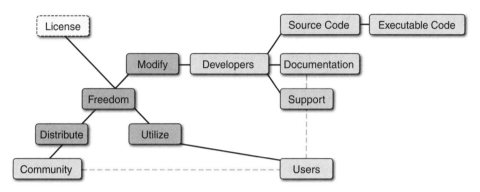

Figure 1.3   Visualize the Open Source community

The graphic in Figure 1.3 highlights the complex combination of elements that make up open source software. You can see that the developers write the source code, create documentation, and provide support. However, the users of the software are often major components in this process as well. In fact, some open source software includes little or no support or documentation from the developer, but rather relies on a strong user base (the community) to provide these critical elements.

Note that the freedoms to modify, distribute, and utilize are also depicted in the diagram in Figure 1.3. Additionally, the software license is what provides these freedoms.

Choosing Open Source Licensing

Ultimately you need to decide whether to license your software as closed source or open source. Part of that decision will be based on specifics regarding licenses, a topic that this chapter covers further. However, you should consider some general benefits to creating open source software:

- **Open source tends to invoke trust.** The reason is that others can see exactly what the software does by looking at the source code.

- **Open source can result in better code and less development time.** With other developers reviewing your code and providing feedback, bug fixes, and improvements are created more rapidly, often at no cost to you.

- **Open source that is "free" can increase the scope of the user base.** More users are willing to try software that is free rather than paying money to test out new software.

- **You can still make money from "free" open source software.** Other available sources of revenue include training, support contracts, and additional services.

Options

Dozens of standard open source licenses and a large number of custom licenses are available. Typically, they fall into one of the following four categories:

- **Standard**—Regular licenses that are often reused for other software products. Typically, these are specific to a country and many of them center around United States or European laws.

- **International**—Regular licenses that are often reused for other software products. Unlike the standard licenses, these licenses are designed to be used throughout the world.

- **Special purpose**—Licenses that are written for specific cases.

- **Nonreusable**—Licenses that are not permitted to be used for any software product besides the product the license was written for.

Key Terms

Regarding open source software licenses, you should understand a couple of key terms. One term is **copyleft**, which ensures intellectual property (IP) can be copied or distributed as open source software. The two forms of copyleft are

- **Strong**—All derived works must maintain original copyleft.

- **Weak**—Derived works don't need to follow the original restrictions.

Another important open source license term is **permissiveness**. This term is related to derived works and whether mixed licenses are allowed. The two forms of permissiveness are

- **Strict**—Limited mixed licenses (no closed source or more permissive licenses)

- **Permissive**—Allows mixed licenses

Examples

The following list describes some of the more popular open source licenses:

- Apache License 2.0:
  - Very permissive
  - Non-copyleft
  - Use for any purpose
  - Distribute and modify
  - Allows derived works
- MIT License:
  - Also known as X11 license
  - Similar to Apache license 2.0

- Very permissive
- Non-copyleft
- Use for any purpose
- Must keep copyright message
- User must agree that no warranty is provided

- GNU General Public License (GPL):
  - Strong copyleft
  - Strict permissiveness
  - All derived works must be GPL
  - Two versions: v2 and v3

- BSD License:
  - Very permissive
  - Non-copyleft
  - Three types:
    - Two-clause—Same as MIT
    - Three-clause—Derived work not endorsed by original holder
    - Four-clause—Advertising must acknowledge original holder

Useful Links

Hopefully, you now have a basic understanding of open source software and licenses. Clearly, the topic is not a simple one, and spending additional time researching which license is the best for your project and organization is important. In addition to consulting a legal expert, you should find the following URL resources helpful:

- **http://choosealicense.com**—This tool uses a series of questions to help you determine which license works best for your situation. It provides a good start, but you should also consult a legal expert before making a final decision.

- **http://fsf.org**—The website for the Free Software Foundation offers a great deal of useful information regarding open source software and licenses.

- **http://opensource.org**—This is another great resource to learn more about open source licenses.

Open Source Humor

Open source: free as in "free speech," not as in "free beer." —Anonymous

Summary

In this chapter you learned the differences between closed and open source software. The concept of free software was also explored. Lastly, you learned about some of the basics of open source licenses. At this point you should be able to start the process of determining what type of license under which to release your software. However, remember that you want to put a lot of time, effort, and thought into this decision before releasing your software because these licenses can have a powerful effect on how your software will be used by the community.

II

Linux Essentials

If you are going to develop software on a Linux-based operating system (OS), then it will be important for you to know how to interact with and manage the OS. The next five chapters are devoted to providing you with a solid foundation in the tools and features of Linux.

These chapters focus specifically on what you should know about Linux as a developer. Linux itself is a huge topic with large volumes devoted to exploring the OS. The goal here is to provide you with what you need to know as a developer, not as a regular end user or administrator.[1]

The next five chapters cover the following:

- The core concepts of the Linux operating system
- What Linux distributions are
- How to manage the Linux filesystem
- Critical Linux commands that all software developers should know
- Essential system administration tasks that will be useful for you to know as a developer

---

1   Certainly, the topics presented will also be useful to these sets of Linux users.

Introduction to Linux

What exactly is Linux? The answer can be a complex one. Technically, Linux is a piece of software called the **kernel**. The kernel handles tasks such as booting the system and interacting with hardware devices. By itself, the kernel doesn't really provide users with any functionality. The rest of the operating system (OS), consisting of the filesystem and a large number of commands, is what provides users with useful features.

Although Linux is technically just the kernel, many people refer to the entire OS as *Linux*. In reality, the collection of software that makes up the OS is known as a **Linux distribution** (also called a **distro**). Many distros are available to choose from, which often results in some confusion for novice Linux users.

What Is a Distribution?

A distribution is a collection of Linux software that is maintained by an organization. Each distribution has features that make it unique. Some distributions are designed for general use whereas others are designed for a very specific use case, like a firewall or a web server.

Picking the distro that works best for you might take some time. The website distrowatch.com can aid you in this endeavor. Additional information is also provided later in this chapter.

Accessing a Linux System

Before you can access a Linux system, you need to have one installed. Because each distro has a different installation program, the steps to installing a distro are not included in this book. However, the following should provide you with enough information to successfully install a distro:

- First consider which distro you want to use. This topic is explored in more detail later in this chapter.

- Consider installing the distro on a Virtual Machine (VM). By using a VM, you can install multiple distros and still use your host operating system. Several VM software choices are available, including VirtualBox, VMware, and Parallels Desktop (for Mac users). Some of these products have free versions, whereas others might charge a license fee.

- During the installation, consider accepting the defaults. Typically, the defaults provide you with the software that you need as a developer. You can always reinstall the distro in the future or add additional software using the tools described in Chapter 6, "System Administration."

Choosing the Right Distribution

Often an organization spends a great deal of time to ensure that it chooses the Linux distribution that best fits the company's needs. Each distro is different, and there isn't a "one distro fits all scenarios" solution. There are many features to take into consideration, including:

- **Cost**—Some distros are entirely free, whereas some charge for support and access to updates.

- **Features**—Some distros provide limited access to software based on the objective of the distro. For example, a security-hardened distro only provides software that has met rigorous security benchmarks.

- **Function**—Some distros are specifically tailored to meet a specific function. For example, a distro might be designed to host database applications.

- **Support**—The organization that creates the distro might provide support, or the support might be completely community sponsored. For most distros used in a corporate environment, the organization that creates and maintains the distro provides support.

Although these might not be all the features you or your organization consider when choosing a distro, the preceding list provides you with an idea of what features are normally considered. Because literally hundreds of distros exist, I recommend exploring http://distrowatch.com, a website devoted to monitoring these distros, their features, and their popularity.

Linux distributions are generally split into three primary families:[2]

- **Debian**—Known to be a favorite of the hard-core Linux geeks, Debian was one of the first Linux distributions. Popular variations of Debian include Ubuntu and Mint.

- **Red Hat**:—Designed to be a commercial distro, Red Hat Linux was introduced shortly after Debian. It is now called Red Hat Enterprise Linux (RHEL). Because it is a commercial distro, payment of a license fee (for support and updates) is required to use RHEL. However, several free Red Hat–based distros exist, including Fedora and CENTOS.

- **Slackware/SUSE**—Slackware was the original "founding father" of this family of distros, but SUSE is the most popular now. SUSE is like RHEL in that it is designed to be a commercial distro. OpenSUSE is a free variation.

---

2 Other families of distros exist, but these three are by far the most often used. If you want to see a "family tree" (somewhat overwhelming), I suggest viewing the following graphic: https://upload.wikimedia .org/wikipedia/commons/1/1b/Linux_Distribution_Timeline.svg

Regarding the information provided in this book, in most cases which distro you use does not matter. However, for some topics the distro does matter. When these situations arise, I provide detailed information regarding the differences between the distros. Otherwise, the examples make use of different distros to highlight that core functionality is largely the same across Linux distributions.[3]

Logging In

Typically, there are three ways to log in to a Linux system:

- **Via the GUI**—On laptops, desktops, and some servers, a GUI-based login appears by default.

- **Via the command line**—Administrators commonly do not install the GUI software on servers because that software is a huge hardware hog (CPU, RAM, and so on). On these servers, you typically see a command-line login.

- **Via the network**—A network-based login could either be via command line (very common) or GUI (not as common). The machine that you log into must have special software installed and enabled to allow this sort of access.

Logging In via the GUI

The software that allows you to log in to a Linux system is called a **display manager**. Several different display manager software programs are available, resulting in a different look and feel for the login screen. In some ways, this is dependent on the distro, because the organization that supports the distro tends to favor one display manager or another. However, an administrator can choose to install a different display manager or configure the appearance of the existing display manager. See Figure 2.1 for an illustration of display managers.

---

3 As a developer, you shouldn't get too hung up on which distro to use. This is often the choice of the company system administrator. Knowing the differences and which ones can affect a developer is what you should focus on (and that is the approach for this book).

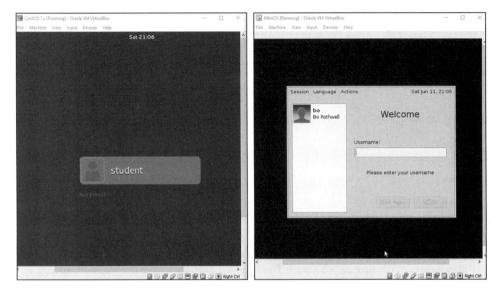

Figure 2.1   The default display manager on CentOS (left) and MintOS (right)

The good news is that regardless of which display manager you use, the basic operation shouldn't change. You either select your user name from a list or type your user name in the dialog box provided. Then you are prompted for your password. As you become more experienced, try exploring other options provided by your display manager, such as shutting down your system.

Logging In via the Command Line

In most cases, you only log in via the command line when the server you are working on has no GUI. However, if your system has a GUI, logging in via a command line is still possible (even if you are working on a virtual machine). Holding down the Ctrl+Alt buttons on your keyboard and pressing the F2 key[4] should provide a command-line login. See Figure 2.2 for an example of a command-line login screen.

---

4 If you are working in a virtual machine, this keystroke combination might vary.

Figure 2.2   A command-line login screen for CentOS

To log out of a command-line environment, type **exit** and then press the Enter key. To return to the GUI screen, press either Ctrl+Alt+F1 or Ctrl+Alt+F2.

Logging In via the Network

You can use a few techniques to log in to a remote system via the network. The techniques that are available depend on two factors: what sort of system you are logging in from and whether you want to log in to a command-line interface (CLI) or GUI:

- **Logging in to a Linux system from a Microsoft Windows system:** You will likely need some additional software because Microsoft Windows doesn't normally provide the software needed to log in to a Linux system. If you want to log in through a CLI, install a Secure Shell (SSH) client program. If you want to log in to a GUI, install a virtual network computing (VNC) client program.[5]

- **Logging in to a Linux system from a Macintosh system:** At its heart, the Macintosh OS is Unix-based, so some client tools should already be available. For example, you should be able to open a terminal window and use the `ssh` command to log in to a Linux system via the CLI. You could also install VNC client software to log in to a Linux system via the GUI.

- **Logging in to a Linux system from a Linux system:** You should be able to use the `ssh` command to log in. A VNC client might also be installed, but if it isn't then contact the administrator.[6]

---

5   Note that normally VNC requires installing a VNC server on the Linux box and configuring it.

6   Unless you have access to root privileges. See Chapter 6 for details regarding software.

In the following example, the "bob" user on the local machine logged in to the machine named "remote" using the "student" account (Note: Instead of a machine name, an IP address can be used):

```
bob@ubuntu:~$ ssh student@remote
The authenticity of host 'remote' can't be established.
ECDSA key fingerprint is 8a:d9:88:b0:e8:05:d6:2b:85:df:53:10:54:66:5f:0f.

Are you sure you want to continue connecting (yes/no)? yes
Warning: Permanently added 'remote' (ECDSA) to the list of known hosts.
student@remote's password:
Welcome to Ubuntu 14.04.2 LTS (GNU/Linux 3.16.0-30-generic x86_64)
student@remote:~$
```

Note the message about the key fingerprint. This is used in the future to verify that you are logging in to the correct system and not some fake machine that has assumed the identity of the remote system. This question only appears the first time you log in to this system.

To return to the local system, execute the exit command.

Using the GUI

The heading "Using the GUI" is a bit misleading because there isn't just one GUI. With Linux, you have your choice of several different **desktops**, each of which provides the same essential functions in different ways in addition to having unique features. A small sample of available desktops includes the following:

- GNOME
- KDE
- Unity+
- Cinnamon
- Xfce
- MATE

With so many desktops available, you might ask yourself "Which one should I use?" To some extent, that question might be answered for you when you choose your Linux distribution. Most distros have a "favored default" desktop which will be installed and used automatically. Although other desktops might be available for the distro, you typically need to install them separately.

In some cases, the developers of the distro might provide you the option of choosing your desktop before you install the distro. For example, consider Figure 2.3, which displays the download links for the Mint distribution.

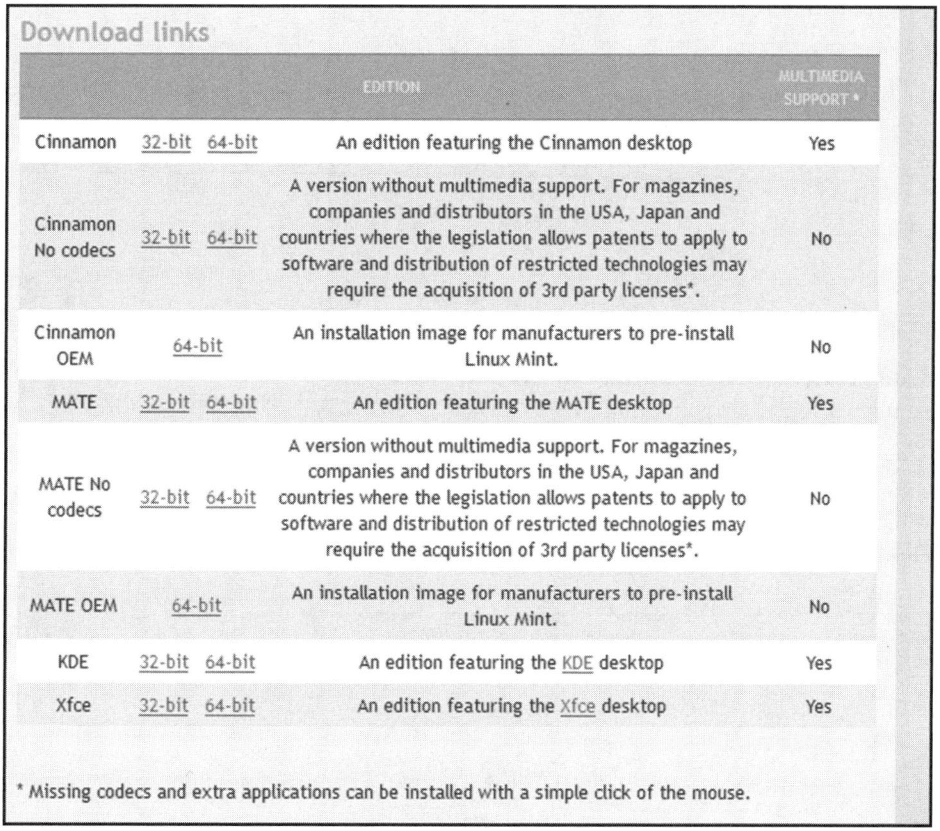

Download links

EDITION			MULTIMEDIA SUPPORT *
Cinnamon	32-bit 64-bit	An edition featuring the Cinnamon desktop	Yes
Cinnamon No codecs	32-bit 64-bit	A version without multimedia support. For magazines, companies and distributors in the USA, Japan and countries where the legislation allows patents to apply to software and distribution of restricted technologies may require the acquisition of 3rd party licenses*.	No
Cinnamon OEM	64-bit	An installation image for manufacturers to pre-install Linux Mint.	No
MATE	32-bit 64-bit	An edition featuring the MATE desktop	Yes
MATE No codecs	32-bit 64-bit	A version without multimedia support. For magazines, companies and distributors in the USA, Japan and countries where the legislation allows patents to apply to software and distribution of restricted technologies may require the acquisition of 3rd party licenses*.	No
MATE OEM	64-bit	An installation image for manufacturers to pre-install Linux Mint.	No
KDE	32-bit 64-bit	An edition featuring the KDE desktop	Yes
Xfce	32-bit 64-bit	An edition featuring the Xfce desktop	Yes

* Missing codecs and extra applications can be installed with a simple click of the mouse.

Figure 2.3   Mint download links

Figure 2.3 shows the different install options provided, primarily divided by the type of desktop. Additionally, a user with administrative access can install multiple desktops on a single system. If there are multiple desktops, you could choose which desktop you want to use before you log in, as demonstrated in Figure 2.4.

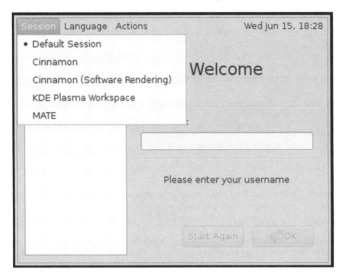

Figure 2.4   Desktop choices at login

After you successfully log in, a desktop appears. The overall look and feel of the desktop varies. However, figuring out where things are on a particular desktop shouldn't take too long. For example, look at Figure 2.5, which displays the default desktops for MintOS.

Figure 2.5   Cinnamon versus MATE desktops

As you can see, the Cinnamon and MATE desktops look very similar. Both provide a menu (bottom left) that enables you to access additional programs and features. Both have quick launch icons and both provide system information (bottom right) such as date/time. The choice comes down to exploring the desktop that you are using rather than memorizing where features reside for a specific desktop.

Basic Command-Line Execution

Although the GUI interface makes using Linux easy, most users and administrators use the command-line environment for system tasks. If you log in to a system via the GUI, you can access the command-line environment by opening a terminal window. The terminal window is a GUI-based program that launches a **shell**, a program that enables you to enter commands. See Figure 2.6 for an example of a terminal window.

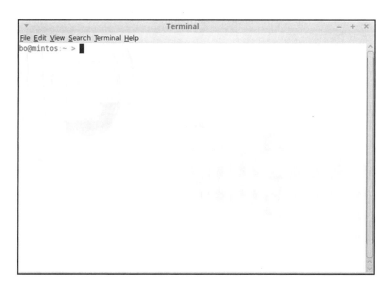

Figure 2.6   Typical terminal window

The most common shell program in Linux is the BASH[7] shell. This book shows BASH shell–based examples.

---

7   BASH stands for Bourne Again SHell. It is based on an older Unix shell named the Bourne Shell.

Command-Line Structure

A command has three components:

- **Command name**—This is just the name of the command.

- **Option(s)**—An option (also referred to as a **flag**) is a predefined value that changes the behavior of the command. The format of options can vary. In some cases, the option begins with a single hyphen followed by a single character; for example: `ls -a`. In other cases, the option begins with two hyphens followed by a word; for example: `ls --all`. In some rare cases, the option is just a single character with no hyphen. The format depends on the command because some commands support the single-hyphen method whereas others support the double-hyphen method (and some support both methods).

- **Arguments**—Arguments are used to provide additional information to the command. This information could be things like a filename, user name, or host name.

See Figure 2.7 for a visual example of the command-line components.

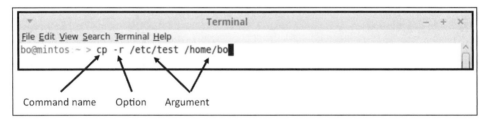

Figure 2.7   Components of a command line

Getting Help

You might be wondering how to tell what options and arguments a command will accept. Several ways exist to display documentation that can help you use a command. One method you could use is the `help` command:

```
bo@mintos:~ > help alias
alias: alias [-p] [name[=value] ... ]
    Define or display aliases.

    Without arguments, 'alias' prints the list of aliases in the reusable
    form 'alias NAME=VALUE' on standard output.

    Otherwise, an alias is defined for each NAME whose VALUE is given.
    A trailing space in VALUE causes the next word to be checked for
    alias substitution when the alias is expanded.
```

```
Options:
  -p     Print all defined aliases in a reusable format

Exit Status:
alias returns true unless a NAME is supplied for which no alias has
been defined.
```

As you can see from the output of the `help alias` command, the command accepts the
`-p` option. Because the option is enclosed within square brackets, the option is not required for
the command to run. Additionally, you can include a `name` or `name=value` argument with the
command. Again, the square brackets indicate that these arguments are not required and that
`name` does not require an `=value` argument.

One drawback of the `help` command is that is only works on built-in shell commands. These
commands are part of the BASH shell, not a separate **executable**.[8] The majority of commands
that you will execute are not built-in shell commands, so the `help` command won't be that
helpful.

However, almost all commands have documentation available via a command called the `man`
command (*man* is short for *manual*). To view a man page for a command, execute `man cmd`,
replacing *cmd* with the command name. For example, to view the man page for the `cal`
command, execute `man cal`.

> **Note**
>
> You will eventually discover that not only commands have man pages. Configuration files and
> other things have man pages, too.

The man page for a given command[9] can be quite large. To facilitate the process of reading the
man page, you can use several keys to move through the document:

- `<spacebar>`—Move down one screen.

- `<ENTER>`—Move down one line.

- `b`—Move back one screen.

- `/term`—Search for term.

- `h`—Display help screen.

- `q`—Quit displaying man page.

Note that these are just a few of the commands that you can use to display a man page.
The h key provides a full list of commands.

---

8 *Executable* is a term that essentially means *program*. If a file can be run like a program, it should
   have the execute permission set.

9 Not only commands have man pages. Configuration files and other items have man pages, too.

> ### Helpful Suggestion
>
> When you are first learning Linux, you might find using man pages to be difficult. The format and syntax of the output can be a challenge to follow. I highly suggest you get as much practice as you can reading man pages. You can do this by looking at the man page for each new command that you learn. Try to find a new feature or option for the new command. Test your ability to run the command with different options based on what you learn from the man page. Learning how to read man pages just comes down to practice.

A typical man page has several different sections. The output begins with a line like the following:

```
CAL(1)                 BSD General Commands Manual                 CAL(1)
```

This indicates the command and the category. This chapter covers man page categories a bit later.

The next section provides a brief description of the command like the following:

```
NAME
     cal, ncal — displays a calendar and the date of Easter
```

After this description, you see a summary of how you can execute the command:

```
SYNOPSIS
     cal [-3hjy] [-A number] [-B number] [[month] year]
     cal [-3hj] [-A number] [-B number] -m month [year]
     ncal [-3bhjJpwySM] [-A number] [-B number] [-s country_code] [[month]
        year]
     ncal [-3bhJeoSM] [-A number] [-B number] [year]
     ncal [-CN] [-H yyyy-mm-dd] [-d yyyy-mm]
```

Recall that square brackets indicate something that isn't required but which is a valid option. For example, you could just run the `cal` command with no options or arguments:

```
bo@mintos:~ > cal
     July 2016
Su Mo Tu We Th Fr Sa
                1  2
 3  4  5  6  7  8  9
10 11 12 13 14 15 16
17 18 19 20 21 22 23
24 25 26 27 28 29 30
31
```

You could also use an option, such as `-3`:

```
bo@mintos:~ > cal -3
      June 2016            July 2016           August 2016
Su Mo Tu We Th Fr Sa  Su Mo Tu We Th Fr Sa  Su Mo Tu We Th Fr Sa
         1  2  3  4                  1  2      1  2  3  4  5  6
 5  6  7  8  9 10 11   3  4  5  6  7  8  9   7  8  9 10 11 12 13
12 13 14 15 16 17 18  10 11 12 13 14 15 16  14 15 16 17 18 19 20
19 20 21 22 23 24 25  17 18 19 20 21 22 23  21 22 23 24 25 26 27
26 27 28 29 30        24 25 26 27 28 29 30  28 29 30 31
                      31
```

However, only options specified in the Synopsis are allowed:

```
bo@mintos:~ > cal -2
cal: invalid option -- '2'
Usage: cal [general options] [-hjy] [[month] year]
       cal [general options] [-hj] [-m month] [year]
       ncal [general options] [-bhJjpwySM] [-s country_code] [[month] year]
       ncal [general options] [-bhJeoSM] [year]
General options: [-NC31] [-A months] [-B months]
For debug the highlighting: [-H yyyy-mm-dd] [-d yyyy-mm]
```

Additionally, you can specify a month and year:

```
bo@mintos:~ > cal 3 1968
    March 1968
Su Mo Tu We Th Fr Sa
             1  2
 3  4  5  6  7  8  9
10 11 12 13 14 15 16
17 18 19 20 21 22 23
24 25 26 27 28 29 30
31
```

The next section provides a greater level of detail regarding how the command and its options work:

```
DESCRIPTION
    The cal utility displays a simple calendar in traditional format and
    ncal offers an alternative layout, more options and the date of Easter.
    The new format is a little cramped but it makes a year fit on a 25x80 terminal.
    If arguments are not specified, the current month is displayed.
    The options are as follows:
    -h      Turns off highlighting of today.
```

Some commands also provide a See Also section that includes a list of related commands:

```
SEE ALSO
    calendar(3), strftime(3)
```

Depending on the man page that you are viewing, you might see additional sections. However, the critical ones have been described here.

Man Page Categories

Many different types of man pages exist. For example, there are man pages for commands that regular users execute and man pages for commands that administrators execute. There are also man pages for libraries (programs used by other programs) and system configuration files.

These different types of man pages are broken into categories,[10] as shown in the man page for the man command:

```
bo@mintos:~ > man man
{output omitted}
        The table below shows the section numbers of the manual followed by
        the types of pages they contain.
        1   Executable programs or shell commands
        2   System calls (functions provided by the kernel)
        3   Library calls (functions within program libraries)
        4   Special files (usually found in /dev)
        5   File formats and conventions eg /etc/passwd
        6   Games
        7   Miscellaneous  (including  macro  packages  and  conventions),
            e.g. man(7), groff(7)
        8   System administration commands (usually only for root)
        9   Kernel routines [Non standard]
```

In most cases, you don't have to worry much about these categories. When you execute the man command, it first searches category 1 for the man page. If it doesn't find it, it then searches the next category.[11] Eventually it finds and displays the man page or displays an error if it can't find the man page in any category:

```
bo@mintos:~ > man nope
No manual entry for nope
```

In some cases you must specify the category. For example, there is a user command named passwd (category 1) and a file format named passwd (category 5). If you execute the man passwd command, the passwd command man page displays. To view the man page for the passwd file, you must execute the man 5 passwd command.

> **Tip**
>
> Most distributions have a GUI-based man page viewer that you might find easier to use. Just type **xman** to launch it.

Info Documentation

In addition to man pages, you might find info documentation helpful. Not all commands and files have info documentation, but for those that do, using it can be easier than using man

---

10 I call them categories, but the man page calls them *sections*. I think this term is confusing because *sections* is also used to refer to different pages within a single man page. So, I call these collections of man pages *categories* to avoid confusion.

11 The following line in the man configuration file determines the order in which man page sections are searched:

```
SECTION   1 1p 8 2 3 3p 4 5 6 7 9 0p n l p o 1x 2x 3x 4x 5x 6x 7x 8x
```

pages. To use an info document, execute the `info` command followed by the command to display; for example, `info ls`.

The documentation found in info pages tends to be more verbose than in man pages. The sections of info pages are also organized differently than man pages. Instead of one long document of text, info pages appear in hyperlinked sections. For example, if you scroll down the document for the `ls` command (use the down-arrow key on your keyboard), you see this:

```
* Menu:
* Which files are listed::
* What information is listed::
* Sorting the output::
* Details about version sort::
* General output formatting::
* Formatting file timestamps::
* Formatting the file names::
```

This is a menu of subcategories you can jump to by placing your cursor on a menu item and pressing the Enter key. After you're in a subcategory, type the letter **u** to go back up one level. To see additional commands, press the H or ? key.

> **Note**
>
> In the help section, press **l** to exit help and return to the info page. Use **q** to quit the info document and return to the command line.

> **Tip**
>
> You can learn a lot from info documentation. Try executing the `info` command with no arguments. Then scroll down to the menu section, pick a category, press the Enter key, and start exploring.

Additional Documentation

In addition to man pages and info documentation, you might find the files in the /usr/share/doc directory to be useful. Chapter 3, "The Filesystem," covers how to navigate the filesystem, which will allow you to access the documentation in the /usr/share/doc directory. For now, just realize that additional documentation exists in this directory (typically it is geared more toward administrators, but some end user documentation exists in this directory, too).

> **Linux Humor**
>
> Ever wonder whether the computer is actually watching you as you are working? Type the `xeyes` command in a terminal window (this only works in a GUI environment) to get the answer to this question.

Summary

In this chapter you learned how to log in to an existing Linux distribution via the command line, a graphical user interface, or across the network. You also learned about different desktops, which provide the look and feel of a GUI. Lastly, you learned how to get additional help using man pages and info documentation.

The Filesystem

Regardless of what you plan to use the Linux distribution for, you need to know how to navigate the filesystem. The filesystem is how the files are structurally organized into directories. Understanding this structure and how to manage the files is critical to using Linux.

Understanding the Filesystem

Typically, new Linux users have some experience in another operating system, such as Microsoft Windows. One of the challenges of using the Linux filesystem is understanding that the layout is likely to be different than what you are used to.

For example, in Microsoft Windows, physical drives are assigned letters, such as C: or F:. They may be visible under the My Computer icon. Linux doesn't use drive letters or a My Computer icon. Instead, all drives, including network drives and removable media, are located under the **root directory**.

The root directory is symbolized by the / character. This character is also used to separate directory and filenames in a **path**. Think of the path as directions to get to a file or directory. For example, the path /home/bob/sample.txt refers to a file named sample.txt that is in the bob directory. The bob directory is under the home directory, which in turn is under the root directory. See Figure 3.1 for a small example of a Linux filesystem.

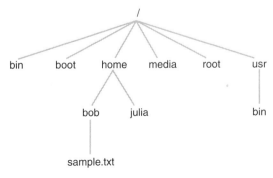

Figure 3.1   Part of a Linux filesystem

Learning the Most Used Directories

Thousands of directories are in a typical Linux filesystem. You should not worry about learning about all of these directories when you first start learning Linux, but some are important enough to learn now:

- **/home**—A user's home directory; each user has a directory under the **/home** directory where she can store her files. This is one of the few places where the user should always have the right to create and manage files.

- **/root**—Root user's home directory; the system administrator account on the system is called the root user. The home directory for the root user isn't under the **/home** directory; instead it is under the **/root** directory.[1]

- **/bin**—Executables (programs); most of the commands you execute as a regular user are placed here or in the **/usr/bin** directory.

- **/usr/bin**—Executables (programs); most of the commands you execute as a regular user are placed here or in the **/bin** directory.

- **/sbin**—Executables (programs) for system administrators; most of the commands you execute as a system administrator are placed here or in the **/usr/sbin** directory.

- **/usr/sbin**—Executables (programs) for system administrators; most of the commands you execute as a system administrators are placed here or in the **/sbin** directory.

- **/media**—Removable media (could also be **/run/media**); this is where you find the files for removable devices, such as CD-ROMs and USB drives.

- **/tmp**—Temporary files; typically, programs store files in this directory rather than placing files in a user's home directory.

Naming Considerations

When you create a file or directory, you should take into consideration the following guidelines:

- Files and directories have same name rules.

- Names are case sensitive. This means that a file named Data.txt is not the same as a file named data.txt.

---

1 I realize this part might be a bit confusing because there are really three "roots" in Linux. The /directory is called the *root directory* because it is the start of the filesystem. The system administrator is called the *root user* and the home directory for the root user is the **/root** *directory*. Linux users often refer to the root directory as the "slash" directory to avoid confusion with /**root** and the root user.

- Special characters are permitted. However, you should avoid using whitespace (space and tab characters) and certain special characters called metacharacters (*, ?, [,], !, $, &, and so on). Metacharacters are special characters to BASH, and they can create problems when used in a file or directory name.

- The / character is used to separate files and directory names: **/usr/share/doc**. As a result, you cannot use the / character in file or directory names.

- Extensions (.txt, .cvs, and so on) are permitted but normally have no special meaning to BASH. In some rare cases they may be required for a specific command, but Linux and the BASH shell typically don't require specific extensions for files. However, extensions are useful for users because understanding the purpose of a file is easier if the extension is provided (some GUI interfaces also make use of extensions to determine which GUI-based program to launch).

- There are some special predefined directory names:

  - ~ —Represents the current user's home directory

  - . —Represents the current working directory (the directory you are working in when using a command-line shell)

  - .. —Represents one level above the current working directory

Navigating the Filesystem

When using the command-line environment, you often need to refer to a directory structure to access a file or subdirectory. For example, you may want to view a file in a specific directory.

When you first open a shell, you are automatically placed in your home directory. The directory you are in is referred to as your *working directory* or current directory. A common task is to switch the working directory to another directory, a process called **change directory**.

A path or pathname is how you refer to a file or directory in the directory structure. The two types of pathnames are

- **Absolute**—A path that always starts from the root directory; for example, **/home/bob/ sample.txt**

- **Relative**—A path that starts from the current directory; for example, if you are in the **/home** directory and want to access the sample.txt file that is under the bob directory (which is under the **/home** directory), you use **bob/sample.txt.**

Note
Absolute paths always start with a / character but relative paths never start with a / character.

To help understand the difference between an absolute and relative path, consider Figure 3.2.

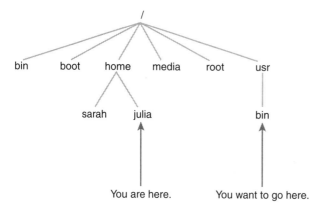

Figure 3.2   Using a pathname, example #1

In this example you are in the /home/julia directory and want to switch to the /usr/bin directory. To switch directories, you can use the cd command, and to view the current directory you can use the pwd[2] directory. The following example demonstrates using an absolute path:

```
julia@mintos:~ > pwd
/home/julia
julia@mintos:~ > cd /usr/bin
julia@mintos:/usr/bin > pwd
/usr/bin
```

Note that the prompt (julia@mintos:/usr/bin) indicates the current directory, so the pwd command isn't always necessary. This isn't always the case because the prompt is customizable.

The next example demonstrates using a relative path to move from the /home/julia directory to the /usr/bin directory. Note that the cd command, when given no arguments, returns you to your home directory:

```
julia@mintos:/usr/bin > cd
julia@mintos:~ > pwd
/home/julia
julia@mintos:~ > cd ../../usr/bin
julia@mintos:/usr/bin > pwd
/usr/bin
```

Why use ..? Because a relative path requires giving directions from the current directory, and you have to tell the cd command to "go up" two levels before going down to the usr and bin directories.

---

2 pwd stands for *print working directory*. In early Unix times, monitors were rare, so output was often sent to an actual printer. Because Unix is the precursor to Linux, many of the commands are named the same.

Clearly, in this case, the absolute path was easier, but that isn't always the case. For example, now consider Figure 3.3.

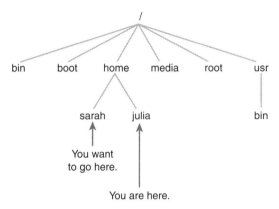

Figure 3.3   Using a pathname, example #2

Now you want to move from the /home/julia directory to the /home/sarah directory. The first example uses an absolute path:

```
julia@mintos:/usr/bin > cd
julia@mintos:~ > cd /home/sarah
julia@mintos:/home/sarah > pwd
/home/sarah
```

Compare the previous example with the following:

```
julia@mintos:/home/sarah > cd
julia@mintos:~ > cd ../sarah
julia@mintos:/home/sarah > pwd
/home/sarah
```

The relative method is easier to use in this case. Consider if you were 20 levels deep in the directory structure and you just wanted to move up one level and down to another subdirectory. Using an absolute path would result in a lot of typing whereas a relative path would be much less work. The lesson here is to know both methods because one is going to be easier than the other most of the time.

Managing the Filesystem

Now that you know how to move from one directory to another, you will want to see what is inside the directories. The ls command lists files in a directory:

```
julia@mintos:~ > cd /etc/sound/events
julia@mintos:/etc/sound/events > ls
mate-battstat_applet.soundlist
```

By default the `ls` command displays all files in the current directory except hidden files. A hidden file has a `.` character at the beginning of the filename. To see all files, including hidden files, use the `-a` option to the `ls` command:

```
julia@mintos:/etc/sound/events > ls -a
.  ..  mate-battstat_applet.soundlist
```

Recall that `.` represents the current directory and `..` represents the directory above the current directories. You will always see these two hidden files[3] regardless of which directory you are in.

To understand why some files are hidden, look at the files in a typical user's home directory:

```
julia@mintos:/etc/sound/events > ls -a ~
.    .bash_history  .bashrc  .config    .gimp-2.8  .local    .profile
..   .bash_logout   .cache   .face.icon  .kde       .mozilla
```

Each of the hidden files (in some cases they are directories) that you see in this output contain information that modifies the user's environment. For example, `.bashrc` and `.profile` modify how the BASH shell works for the current user. The `.mozilla` directory contains configuration settings for Firefox, a web browser provided by the Mozilla Foundation.

How could you tell if `.bashrc` was a file or `.mozilla` was a directory? Use the `-l` option:

```
julia@mintos:/etc/sound/events > ls -a -l ~
total 48
drwxr-xr-x 8 julia julia 4096 Jul 14 17:26 .
drwxr-xr-x 5 root  root  4096 Jul 14 17:26 ..
-rw------- 1 julia julia   72 Jul 14 17:26 .bash_history
-rw-r--r-- 1 julia julia  220 Apr  8  2014 .bash_logout
-rw-r--r-- 1 julia julia 1452 Jan  5  2016 .bashrc
drwx------ 3 julia julia 4096 Jul 14 17:12 .cache
drwxr-xr-x 6 julia julia 4096 Jun  5 15:59 .config
lrwxrwxrwx 1 julia julia    5 Jun  5 14:40 .face.icon -> .face
drwxr-xr-x 2 julia julia 4096 Jan  5  2016 .gimp-2.8
drwxr-xr-x 3 julia julia 4096 Jan  5  2016 .kde
drwxr-xr-x 3 julia julia 4096 Jan  5  2016 .local
drwxr-xr-x 3 julia julia 4096 Jan  5  2016 .mozilla
-rw-r--r-- 1 julia julia  675 Apr  8  2014 .profile
```

When you use the `-l` option, each line describes detailed information for a file. See Figure 3.4 for a demonstration of the details that are provided.

---

3 You may be wondering if I accidently called `.` and `..` a file. In Linux, everything is considered a file, including directories. A directory is just a special file that holds other directories. Normally I would refer to these as directories, but I wanted to take the opportunity to make this point as it could prove important as you dive deeper into Linux.

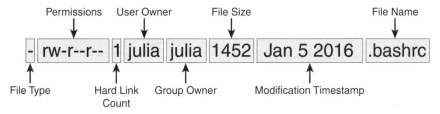

Figure 3.4   Details of the `ls -l` command

The details of the information provided by the `ls -l` command:

- **File type**—d means this is a directory whereas - means it is a plain file. There are additional file types, but these are the primary two you should know.[4]

- **Permissions**—These are used to allow or disallow access to the file. Chapter 4, "Essential Commands" covers permissions.

- **Hard link count**—A more advanced topic normally reserved for system administrators, this is a file that is hard linked and shares the same data block space with another filename.

- **User owner**—The user who owns the file has special access to the file. For example, only the user owner (and the root user) can change the permissions of a file.

- **Group owner**—Group owners have special access to the file via permissions.

- **File size**—The size of the file in bytes.[5]

- **Modification timestamp**—The date and time the file was last modified.[6]

- **Filename**—The name of the file.

> **Note**
>
> You can use many other options with the `ls` command. Recall the suggestion from Chapter 2, "Introduction to Linux," regarding viewing the man page for each new command that you learn. This would be an excellent time to make use of that suggestion!

---

4 You may also want to know about `l`, which stands for **symbolic link**. A symbolic link is a file that points to another file. If you have experience in Windows, symbolic links are akin to shortcuts on your desktop.

5 File sizes in bytes can be difficult to comprehend, especially for large files. Consider including the `-h` option to show file sizes in "human readable" sizes.

6 If the file was last modified within the past six months, the timestamp includes a month, day, and time. If the file was last modified more than six months ago, the time is replaced with the year.

Managing Directories

To create a new directory, use the `mkdir` command:

```
julia@mintos:~ > ls
julia@mintos:~ > mkdir data
julia@mintos:~ > ls -l
total 4
drwxrwxr-x 2 julia julia 4096 Jul 15 09:34 data
```

Note a situation in which this could fail:

```
julia@mintos:~ > ls
data
julia@mintos:~ > mkdir test/samples
mkdir: cannot create directory 'test/samples': No such file or directory
```

This failure occurs because to make the samples directory in the test directory, the test directory must exist. To make both the samples and test directory, use the `-p` option to the `mkdir` command:

```
julia@mintos:~ > ls
data
julia@mintos:~ > mkdir -p test/samples
julia@mintos:~ > ls
data  test
julia@mintos:~ > ls test
samples
```

To delete a directory that is empty, use the `rmdir` command:

```
julia@mintos:~ > ls
data  test
julia@mintos:~ > rmdir data
julia@mintos:~ > ls
test
```

The `rmdir` command only works on empty directories:

```
julia@mintos:~ > ls
test
julia@mintos:~ > rmdir test
rmdir: failed to remove 'test': Directory not empty
```

To delete an entire directory structure, including all the files and subdirectories, use the `rm` command with the `-r` option:

```
julia@mintos:~ > ls
test
julia@mintos:~ > rm -r test
julia@mintos:~ > ls
julia@mintos:~ >
```

> **Note**
> The `rm` command is normally used to delete files. With the `-r` option, it can delete directories and files.

Be careful when using the `rm -r` command. You could accidentally delete files that you really need to keep. Consider using the `-i` option when executing the `rm -r` command because this enables you to pick which files to delete. When prompted, answer **y** for yes and **n** for no:[7]

```
julia@mintos:~ > rm -ri events
rm: descend into directory 'events'? y
rm: remove regular file 'events/mate-battstat_applet.soundlist'? y
rm: remove directory 'events'? n
```

Managing Files

To copy a file, use the `cp` command. You should have two arguments: what file to copy and where to copy it:

```
julia@mintos:~ > ls
events
julia@mintos:~ > cp /etc/hosts .
julia@mintos:~ > ls
events  hosts
```

Recall that `.` represents the current directory.

Be careful when using the `cp` command because you can accidentally overwrite an existing file. This happens when the destination (where to copy the file) contains a file with the exact same name as an existing file:

```
ulia@mintos:~ > ls -l hosts
-rw-r--r-- 1 julia julia 221 Jul 15 10:47 hosts
julia@mintos:~ > cp /etc/passwd hosts
julia@mintos:~ > ls -l hosts
-rw-r--r-- 1 julia julia 2074 Jul 15 10:52 hosts
```

You can tell that the original file was overwritten because the file size changed (221 bytes to 2074 bytes) and the modification timestamp changed. To avoid overwriting an existing file, use the `-i` option:

```
julia@mintos:~ > ls -l hosts
-rw-r--r-- 1 julia julia 221 Jul 15 10:56 hosts
julia@mintos:~ > cp -i /etc/passwd hosts
cp: overwrite 'hosts'? n
julia@mintos:~ > ls -l hosts
-rw-r--r-- 1 julia julia 221 Jul 15 10:56 hosts
```

---

7 The `rm -ri` command is the same as the `rm -ir` command, which is the same as the `rm -r -i` command. In most cases, single character options can be combined and order doesn't matter.

The -i option stands for "interactive" mode and prompts you if the cp command will end up overwriting an existing file.

Some additional useful commands to manage files include the following:

- mv—Used to move files or directories

- rm—Used to delete files

- touch—Creates an empty file or updates the modification timestamp of an existing file

Wildcards

Suppose you want to copy all the files that end in .conf from the /etc directory to a directory called config in your home directory. You look in the /etc directory and realize that there are about 20 of these files. You don't want to have to type in the name of each file. This is a case in which you want to use wildcards.

With wildcards, you can make use of special characters to match file or directory names. For example, you can list all the files in the /etc directory that end in .conf by executing the following command:[8]

```
julia@mintos:~ > ls -d /etc/*.conf
/etc/adduser.conf           /etc/insserv.conf          /etc/pam.conf
/etc/apg.conf               /etc/inxi.conf             /etc/pnm2ppa.conf
/etc/avserver.conf          /etc/kernel-img.conf       /etc/request-key.conf
/etc/blkid.conf             /etc/kerneloops.conf       /etc/resolv.conf
/etc/brltty.conf            /etc/ld.so.conf            /etc/rsyslog.conf
/etc/ca-certificates.conf   /etc/libao.conf            /etc/sensors3.conf
/etc/casper.conf            /etc/libaudit.conf         /etc/sysctl.conf
/etc/colord.conf            /etc/logrotate.conf        /etc/ts.conf
/etc/debconf.conf           /etc/ltrace.conf           /etc/ucf.conf
/etc/deluser.conf           /etc/mke2fs.conf           /etc/uniconf.conf
/etc/fuse.conf              /etc/mtools.conf           /etc/updatedb.conf
/etc/gai.conf               /etc/netscsid.conf         /etc/usb_modeswitch.conf
/etc/hdparm.conf            /etc/nsswitch.conf         /etc/wodim.conf
/etc/host.conf              /etc/ntp.conf              /etc/wvdial.conf
```

The * character represents "zero or more characters in a filename." So, you are asking to see files in the /etc directory that begin with "zero or more characters, followed by .conf." Using the * character, you can copy these files into a directory under your home directory (don't worry if you get an error message for some of the files): [9]

---

8   You may be wondering why I used the -d option with the ls command. Be patient; I will explain this soon.

9   The cp command in this example generates some error messages because of file permission issues. Chapter 4 covers file permissions. For now, don't worry if your command generates a few error messages like these.

```
julia@mintos:~ > mkdir config
julia@mintos:~ > cp /etc/*.conf config
cp: cannot open '/etc/fuse.conf' for reading: Permission denied
cp: cannot open '/etc/wvdial.conf' for reading: Permission denied
julia@mintos:~ > ls config
adduser.conf          gai.conf          logrotate.conf    resolv.conf
apg.conf              hdparm.conf       ltrace.conf       rsyslog.conf
avserver.conf         host.conf         mke2fs.conf       sensors3.conf
blkid.conf           insserv.conf      mtools.conf       sysctl.conf
brltty.conf          inxi.conf         netscsid.conf     ts.conf
ca-certificates.conf kernel-img.conf   nsswitch.conf     ucf.conf
casper.conf          kerneloops.conf   ntp.conf          uniconf.conf
colord.conf          ld.so.conf        pam.conf          updatedb.conf
debconf.conf         libao.conf        pnm2ppa.conf      usb_modeswitch.conf
deluser.conf         libaudit.conf     request-key.conf  wodim.conf
```

Use the ? character to represent a single character. So, to display any files in the /etc directory that have filenames that are exactly four characters in length, execute the following command:

```
julia@mintos:~ > ls -d /etc/????
/etc/acpi  /etc/dkms  /etc/init  /etc/mono  /etc/perl  /etc/udev
/etc/cups  /etc/dpkg  /etc/kde4  /etc/mtab  /etc/sgml  /etc/xrdb
/etc/dhcp  /etc/gimp  /etc/ldap  /etc/newt  /etc/skel
```

The ? character will match any single character. If you want to match a specific character, you can use a set of square brackets, []. For example, to match a file in the /etc directory that begins with an *a*, *b*, or *c* character, execute the following command:

```
julia@mintos:~ > ls -d /etc/[abc]*
/etc/acpi            /etc/avserver.conf           /etc/chatscripts
/etc/adduser.conf    /etc/bash.bashrc             /etc/chromium-browser
/etc/adjtime         /etc/bash_completion         /etc/colord.conf
/etc/akonadi         /etc/bash_completion.d       /etc/compizconfig
/etc/alternatives    /etc/bindresvport.blacklist  /etc/console
/etc/anacrontab      /etc/blkid.conf              /etc/console-setup
/etc/apg.conf        /etc/blkid.tab               /etc/cracklib
/etc/apm             /etc/bluetooth               /etc/cron.d
/etc/apparmor        /etc/brlapi.key              /etc/cron.daily
/etc/apparmor.d      /etc/brltty                  /etc/cron.hourly
/etc/apport          /etc/brltty.conf             /etc/cron.monthly
/etc/apt             /etc/ca-certificates         /etc/crontab
/etc/at.deny         /etc/ca-certificates.conf    /etc/cron.weekly
/etc/at-spi2         /etc/calendar                /etc/cups
/etc/avahi           /etc/casper.conf             /etc/cupshelpers
```

Using a Range in [ ]

Note that [abc] is the same as [a-c]. Using a - enables you to specify a range of permitted characters. Just be sure it is a valid range according to the ASCII text table. You can view this table by executing the command man ascii.

The wildcard characters are not specific to any particular command. Instead, they are part of the BASH shell. This is important to note because it means you can use wildcard characters with any command. The BASH shell interprets the wildcard characters before the command runs.

In fact, the command doesn't even know that wildcard characters are being used. For example, consider the following command:

```
julia@mintos:~ > ls -d /etc/[xyz]*
/etc/xdg  /etc/xemacs21  /etc/xml  /etc/xrdb  /etc/zsh
```

The argument /etc/[xyz]* isn't passed into the ls command. BASH first converts the wildcard pattern into the filename(s) that match. So, if you execute the ls -d /etc/[xyz]* command, the command that is really executed is the ls -d /etc/xdg /etc/xemacs21 /etc/xml /etc/xrdb /etc/zsh command.

This is also why when you use wildcards with the ls command, you should use the -d option. When the ls command runs and is passed a directory name as an argument, the contents of the directory are listed:

```
julia@mintos:~ > ls /etc/xdg
autostart  menus  Trolltech.conf  user-dirs.conf  user-dirs.defaults
```

When you use wildcard characters, some of the matching files could actually be directories. This produces output that you likely don't want to receive:

```
julia@mintos:~ > ls /etc/[xyz]*
/etc/zsh

/etc/xdg:
autostart  menus  Trolltech.conf  user-dirs.conf  user-dirs.defaults

/etc/xemacs21:
site-start.d

/etc/xml:
catalog            docbook-xml.xml.old  rarian-compat.xml  xml-core.xml
catalog.old        docbook-xsl.xml      sgml-data.xml       xml-core.xml.old
docbook-xml.xml  docbook-xsl.xml.old  sgml-data.xml.old

/etc/xrdb:
Editres.ad  Emacs.ad  General.ad  Motif.ad  Tk.ad  Xaw.ad
```

To avoid having the contents of all of these directories, use the -d option to the ls command. The -d option tells the ls command "if any argument happens to be a directory, don't display what is in that directory, just show the directory name."

Redirection

Suppose you run a command and you decide that you want to store the output of the command into a file for future use. In a situation like this, you can use a process called **redirection**. The idea is to redirect the output of a command into a file or another process. You can also redirect the input to a command from a file.

Each command has three data streams:

- **Standard input (stdin)**—The data that is sent into the command. This is not an argument but rather additional information that is being sent into a command. Typically, this data comes from a user who is executing the command. The user provides this data via the keyboard. This input could be redirected from a file or another process.

- **Standard output (stdout)**—The data that is sent from the command when all goes well. Typically, this appears on the screen, but it can be sent to a file or to another command.

- **Standard error (stderr)**—The data that is sent from the command when an error occurs. Typically, this appears on the screen, but it can be sent to a file or to another command.

To redirect stdout, use the > character after the command:

```
julia@mintos:~ > cal 12 2000 > mycal
julia@mintos:~ > cat mycal
   December 2000
Su Mo Tu We Th Fr Sa
                1  2
 3  4  5  6  7  8  9
10 11 12 13 14 15 16
17 18 19 20 21 22 23
24 25 26 27 28 29 30
31
```

Note

You use the `cat` command to display small files; it is covered in Chapter 4.

You use the > character when you want to create a new file or overwrite the contents of an existing file. If you want to append to an existing file, use two > characters:

```
julia@mintos:~ > cat mycal
   December 2000
Su Mo Tu We Th Fr Sa
                1  2
 3  4  5  6  7  8  9
10 11 12 13 14 15 16
17 18 19 20 21 22 23
24 25 26 27 28 29 30
31
```

```
julia@mintos:~ > date >> mycal
julia@mintos:~ > cat mycal
   December 2000
Su Mo Tu We Th Fr Sa
                1  2
 3  4  5  6  7  8  9
10 11 12 13 14 15 16
17 18 19 20 21 22 23
24 25 26 27 28 29 30
31
Sun Jul 17 07:24:51 PDT 2016
```

The output of the `cal` and `date` commands in the previous examples is considered standard output because the command ran successfully. Notice that if a command fails for some reason (such as improper options or arguments), the command's output is not redirected to a file when you use the `>` or `>>` characters:

```
julia@mintos:~ > cal -5 12 2000 > mycal
cal: invalid option -- '5'
Usage: cal [general options] [-hjy] [[month] year]
       cal [general options] [-hj] [-m month] [year]
       ncal [general options] [-bhJjpwySM] [-s country_code] [[month] year]
       ncal [general options] [-bhJeoSM] [year]
General options: [-NC31] [-A months] [-B months]
For debug the highlighting: [-H yyyy-mm-dd] [-d yyyy-mm]
julia@mintos:~ > cat mycal
julia@mintos:~ >
```

When an error occurs, the command sends output to stderr. You can redirect this output by using the `2>` characters:[10]

```
julia@mintos:~ > cal -5 12 2000 > mycal 2> error
julia@mintos:~ > cat error
cal: invalid option -- '5'
Usage: cal [general options] [-hjy] [[month] year]
       cal [general options] [-hj] [-m month] [year]
       ncal [general options] [-bhJjpwySM] [-s country_code] [[month] year]
       ncal [general options] [-bhJeoSM] [year]
General options: [-NC31] [-A months] [-B months]
For debug the highlighting: [-H yyyy-mm-dd] [-d yyyy-mm]
```

---

10 It might seem strange that you use `>` to redirect stdout and `2>` to redirect stderr. However, the official way you redirect stdout is by using the `1>` characters. Because stdout is more commonly redirected than stderr, the BASH shell permits you to drop the `1` before the `>` character.

Important notes regarding redirecting stderr include the following:

- The `2>` characters either create a new file or overwrite the contents of an existing file. To append stderr messages to an existing file, use `2>>`.

- To send all output, both stdout and stderr, to a single file, use the following[11]:

  ```
  cmd > file 2>&1
  ```

- Sometimes you will want to run a command without seeing any of the error messages. To discard the output of a command, send it to the file. This file is called the "bit bucket" or "black hole" because whatever you send to the file will be discarded.

Redirecting stdout and stderr is a fairly common practice. Conversely, redirecting stdin (standard input) is much rarer. Before demonstrating redirecting stdin, consider the following exercise, which demonstrates where stdin comes from by default. Start by executing the following command:

```
julia@mintos:~ > tr 'a-z' 'A-Z'
```

It looks like this program hangs, but it is just waiting for stdin. You can provide stdin from the keyboard. For example, type a sentence and then press the Enter key:

```
julia@mintos:~ > tr 'a-z' 'A-Z'
today is a good day to learn linux
TODAY IS A GOOD DAY TO LEARN LINUX
```

You can see what the `tr` command does with the input. It translates all lowercase letters to uppercase letters. Clearly, performing this task on a file, not input from the keyboard, would be much more useful. Unfortunately, the `tr` command doesn't allow you to provide a filename (By the way, to stop the current `tr` command, hold down the Ctrl key and press the C key. This is normally written as Ctrl+C or just ^C):

```
julia@mintos:~ > tr 'a-z' 'A-Z' mycal
tr: extra operand 'mycal'
Try 'tr --help' for more information.
```

The `tr` command only accepts input from stdin. So, you need to tell the BASH shell to pull stdin data from a file rather than from the keyboard. To do this, use the < character:

```
julia@mintos:~ > tr 'a-z' 'A-Z' < mycal
    DECEMBER 2000
SU MO TU WE TH FR SA
                1  2
 3  4  5  6  7  8  9
10 11 12 13 14 15 16
17 18 19 20 21 22 23
24 25 26 27 28 29 30
31
```

---

11 You can also use the following syntax in the BASH shell: `cmd &> file`

Note that the output of the tr command is sent to the screen via stdout. Essentially, it is now lost, but you can also run the command and redirect stdout to a file (just make sure it is a different file than the original):

```
julia@mintos:~ > tr 'a-z' 'A-Z' < mycal > mynewcal
julia@mintos:~ > cat mynewcal
   DECEMBER 2000
SU MO TU WE TH FR SA
                1  2
 3  4  5  6  7  8  9
10 11 12 13 14 15 16
17 18 19 20 21 22 23
24 25 26 27 28 29 30
31
```

Most commands that require input accept a file as an argument, so you won't redirect stdin nearly as often as you will redirect stdout or stderr. However, some advanced scenarios exist in which knowing how to redirect stdin is very useful.

You can also redirect stdout into another command instead of a file. This is useful because many of the commands on the system perform filtering or **paging** functions.[12]

For example, execute the following command: ls -l /etc. Typically, the /etc directory contains hundreds of files, so the output of this ls command will quickly scroll by on the screen. This can make viewing large amounts of information difficult. The solution is to send the output of the ls command into another command that will display one page of data at a time: ls -l /etc | more.

The | character is used to redirect stdout to another command. It becomes the stdin of the command to the right of the | character, in this case the more command, which displays data one page at a time. Chapter 4 covers the more command in greater detail. For now, use the spacebar to scroll one page at a time and the q character to end displaying the output and return to a prompt.

This process, called **piping**, is useful when you work in a command-line environment. Understanding it might be a bit difficult if this is your first exposure, so a couple of diagrams might be helpful. First consider Figure 3.5, which shows how the ls command functions when piping is not used.

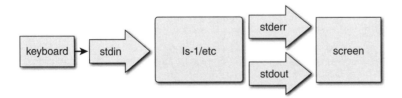

Figure 3.5   The ls -l command without piping

---

12 Paging is displaying one page or screen of data at a time.

Now compare this to Figure 3.6 in which the stdout from the `ls` command is piped into the `more` command.

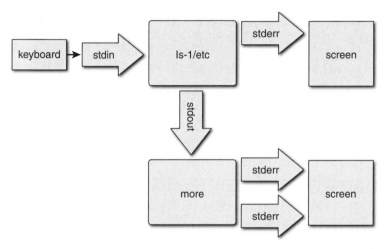

Figure 3.6   The `ls -l` command with piping

Notice in Figure 3.6 that only stdout is redirected when using piping. The command's stderr will still be displayed on the screen directly.

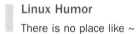 **Linux Humor**
There is no place like ~

Summary

In this chapter you learned how to manage the Linux filesystem, including how to handle files and directories. The concept of using wildcards to match file and directory names was introduced. In addition, you learned how to redirect the output and input of commands into either files or other commands.

4

Essential Commands

A major component of working on a Linux system is the command-line environment. Often referred to as the command-line interface (CLI), this component of Linux provides a huge variety of tools. As a developer, you don't have to learn how to use all of these tools, but knowing key command-line tools makes the task of developing code a much easier one.

This chapter focuses on the essential Linux commands that all developers should know. This chapter builds on what you learned in Chapter 2 (basic command-line execution) and Chapter 3 (filesystem management commands) and provides you with a solid foundation for working in a Linux command-line shell environment.

Command-Line Tools

At this point you might be wondering "Why command-line tools?" If your experience is primarily with GUI-based systems, such as Microsoft Windows, you might consider the CLI something that belongs in the dark ages of computing. However, good reasons exist for why command-line tools have their place on modern operating systems:

- **Stability:** Many Linux commands were derived from Unix and are essentially decades old. This stability means Linux developers can focus on making more tools rather than reinventing features that already exist.[1]

- **Speed of development:** Developing command-line tools takes much less time than developing GUI-based tools. As a result, the developers who create Linux tools can create command-line tools faster than GUI-based tools.

- **Scripting:** Suppose you want to execute a set of instructions each day. With a GUI-based tool, you would have to do this manually every day. With command-line tools, you can create a script, which is a collection of command-line tools. You will learn more about this in Chapters 7 and 8.

---

1 It also means that you can wake up a Unix developer who was cryogenically frozen in the 1970s and that developer would already understand the basics of working in Linux. Note that the process of waking up cryogenically frozen developers is beyond the scope of this book.

- **Speed of use:** Although you might not believe this initially, you can actually perform tasks quicker on the command line (especially if you are good at typing on a keyboard). Normally, GUI-based tools require both mouse and keyboard input (imagine doing a "save as" of a document). This slows you down as you have to take your hands off the keyboard to use the mouse (or vice versa). Additionally, in Linux you can quickly re-execute previous commands as well as bring up previous commands, edit them, and execute them. After you get used to all of this, you can accomplish system tasks more quickly.

- **Power:** You can combine commands to do things the original creator never conceived of doing and complete tasks in a much more elegant, efficient, and useful way.

How Many Commands Are There?

As an instructor I have often been asked by students, "Can you provide a full list of all the Linux commands?" I often wonder whether astronomers are ever asked the similar question, "Can you provide a full list of all the stars in the sky?"

Although there are not 100 billion Linux commands, there are many more than you want to commit to a single list. A typical "small" installation with just the basic software will result in at least a couple thousand commands. It isn't unusual to have more than 10,000 commands on a system that has many of the optional software packages installed.

My advice: Don't worry about learning about all the commands. Focus on the ones that help you do your job (in this case, those that help you develop code).

Viewing Files

A good number of the files on a Linux filesystem are text files. As a result, a lot of commands exist to view the contents of text files. This section introduces many of these files.

The `file` Command

Before you attempt to view the contents of a file, first make sure the contents are in text format and not some other format. Linux supports many file types besides just text files, including compressed files, files that contain executable code, and database formatted files. To determine what type of contents a file contains, execute the following `file` command:

```
[student@localhost ~]$ file /usr/share/dict/linux.words
/usr/share/dict/linux.words: ASCII text
[student@localhost ~]$ file /bin/ls
/bin/ls: ELF 64-bit LSB executable, x86-64, version 1 (SYSV), dynamically linked (uses
shared libs), for GNU/Linux 2.6.32, BuildID[sha1]=aa7ff68f13de25936a098016243ce57c3c9
82e06, stripped
[student@localhost ~]$ file /usr/share/doc/sed-4.2.2/sedfaq.txt.gz
/usr/share/doc/sed-4.2.2/sedfaq.txt.gz: gzip compressed data, was "sedfaq.txt", from
Unix, last modified: Mon Feb 10 09:11:16 2014, max compression
```

If the output of the file command includes "text", such as with the command `file` `/usr/share/dict/linux.words`, then you can use the commands described in this section to view its contents. However, you don't want to use these commands to view ELF 64-bit, gzip compressed data, or other non-text file types. In most cases, viewing these files will result in "garbage" being displayed on your screen. In some cases it can even mess up your terminal window.[2]

The `cat` Command

For the times when you want to view the contents of a small file, the `cat` command (short for concatenate) works well:

```
[student@localhost ~]$ cat /etc/cgrules.conf
# /etc/cgrules.conf
#The format of this file is described in cgrules.conf(5)
#manual page.
#
# Example:
#<user>         <controllers>    <destination>
#@student       cpu,memory       usergroup/student/
#peter          cpu              test1/
#%              memcry           test2/
# End of file
*:iscsid net_prio cgdcb-4-3260
```

A useful `cat` option for developers is the -n option, which is used to number lines. This can be helpful when viewing source code scripts that execute with an error message, as shown in Listing 4.1.[3]

Listing 4.1   **The `cat` -n command**

```
[student@localhost ~]$ ./display.sh
Report of current contents of /etc:
./display.sh: line 5: [-d: command not found
[student@localhost ~]$ cat -n display.sh
     1 #!/usr/bin/bash
     2
     3 echo "Report of current contents of /etc:"
     4
     5 if [-d /etc]
     6 then
     7     echo -n "Number of directories: "
```

---

2 If you view a non-text file accidentally and it messes up your terminal display with "garbage" characters, type the `reset` command and press the Enter key. Don't worry if it looks like garbage when you type the command, it will execute properly and fix your terminal display.

3 Are you wondering what this script actually does? Keep reading this chapter to find out!

```
 8    ls -l /etc | grep "^d" | wc -l
 9    echo -n "Number of links: "
10    ls -l /etc | grep "^l" | wc -l
11    echo -n "Number of regular files: "
12    ls -l /etc | grep "^-" | wc -l
13 fi
```

The `more` and `less` Commands

The problem with the `cat` command comes about when trying to display large files. You will discover that it doesn't pause at any point during display of the file, but rather it scrolls through the file as if you had some superhero speed-reading skill.

To pause the display while displaying the contents of large files, use the `more` or the `less` commands:

```
[student@localhost ~]$ more /usr/share/dict/linux.words
[student@localhost ~]$ less /usr/share/dict/linux.words
```

> ### Why Both `more` and `less`?
>
> Why two commands that do essentially the same thing? The `more` command is the original and the `less` command is an "improved version" of the `more` command (hence giving rise to the joke "less does more than more"[4]).
>
> In reality, the extra features provided by the `less` command are less-often used features, at least for most Linux users. The `more` command is also useful because it is on every Linux (and Unix, MacOS, and Windows) system in the world. The `less` command is part of an optional software package and not available by default on many systems.

The `more` and `less` commands are also useful for pausing the display of a command that produces a large amount of output. Use the pipe character that was covered in Chapter 3 to send the output of a command to the `more` command:

```
[student@localhost ~]$ ls -l /etc | more
```

While viewing a file with the `more` or `less` command, you can use commands to control the display. For example, press the spacebar to scroll down one screen of data. Use the Enter key to move down one line at a time.

See the following for useful commands to control the display while using the `more` or `less` commands:

- Spacebar   Scroll down one screen
- Enter   Scroll down one line
- h   Displays help screen (summary of commands)

---

4 This is about as funny as Linux jokes get. I apologize for all future Linux jokes made throughout this book.

- q   Exit

- /{*pattern*}   Search for {pattern}

- n   Find next occurrence of previous {pattern}

- :f   Displays filename and current line number

The `head` and `tail` Commands

Sometimes you might want to display only the top or bottom part of a file. For example, you might want to look at the comments at the top of a source code file. Or, you want to display recent entries of a log file, which are normally placed at the bottom of the file. For these situations, use the `head` and `tail` commands.

By default, these commands display ten lines. For example, Listing 4.2 demonstrates displaying the top ten lines of the `/usr/share/dict/linux.words` file.

Listing 4.2   **The head command**

```
[student@localhost ~]$ head /usr/share/dict/linux.words
1080
10-point
10th
11-point
12-point
16-point
18-point
1st
20-point
```

Use the `-n` option to specify how many lines to display. For example, the command `tail -n 5 /etc/passwd` displays the last five lines of the `/etc/passwd` file.

The `wc` command

To display statistical information about a file, including the number of lines, words, and characters in the file, use the `wc` command:

```
[student@localhost ~]$ wc display.sh
   13   59 291 display.sh
```

The output displayed is the number of lines (13), the number of words (59), and number of bytes (291) that are in the `display.sh` file. Because `display.sh` is a text file, the number of bytes is actually the number of characters (1 character = 1 byte).

You can limit or modify the output of the wc command by using the following options:

- -c Display number of bytes
- -m Display number of characters (different than number of bytes for non-text files)
- -l Display number of lines
- -w Display the number of words

Finding Files

There is bound to be a time when you have misplaced a file or just cannot remember where a file is stored. In these cases, you can turn to the locate or find commands to search the system for the missing file.

The locate Command

Early each morning a database is created that contains a list of all files and directories on the system. The locate command is used to search this database. For example, to find the linux. words file, execute the following command:

```
[student@localhost ~]$ locate linux.words
/usr/share/dict/linux.words
```

The locate command searches for any file that contains the pattern "linux.words," which might result in more output than expected:

```
[student@localhost ~]$ locate words | head
/etc/libreport/forbidden_words.conf
/etc/libreport/ignored_words.conf
/usr/include/bits/wordsize.h
/usr/lib64/perl5/CORE/keywords.h
/usr/lib64/perl5/bits/wordsize.ph
```

The find Command

The locate command is useful, but it does have a couple of drawbacks. One drawback is that it searches a database that was created earlier in the day. So, if you lose a file that you created today, the locate command won't be able to find this file.

The find command searches the live filesystem, which takes more time than using the locate command (searching databases is much faster), but it does find files that are currently on the filesystem. The syntax for the find command is as follows:

```
find [starting location] [option/arguments]
```

For example, to search for the linux.words file, execute the following command:

```
[student@localhost ~]$ find /usr -name linux.words
find: '/usr/lib/firewalld': Permission denied
find: '/usr/lib64/Pegasus': Permission denied
```

```
/usr/share/dict/linux.words
find: '/usr/share/Pegasus/scripts': Permission denied
find: '/usr/share/polkit-1/rules.d': Permission denied
find: '/usr/libexec/initscripts/legacy-actions/auditd': Permission denied
```

Note the error messages that appear are because directories existed that the current user was not allowed to search. This is one of the reasons why you want to start your search in a subdirectory, not in the / directory. Another reason is because a search of the entire filesystem, starting from the root directory, might take a lot of time.

You can prevent these error messages by using the redirection method discussed in Chapter 3:

```
[student@localhost ~]$ find /usr -name linux.words 2> /dev/null
/usr/share/dict/linux.words
```

Another advantage of the `find` command over the `locate` command is that the `find` command can search using a variety of different file attributes. For example, you can search for files that are owned by specific users:

```
find /home -user student
```

Commonly used `find` options for specifying what to search for include the following:

- `-mmin` *n*—Display files that were modified *n* minutes ago. Use `-mmin +n` to specify "more than *n* minutes ago" or `-mmin -n` to specify "less than *n* minutes ago."

- `-mtime` *n*—Display files that were modified *n* days ago (technically *n**24 hours ago). Can use `+n` and `-n` like the `-mmin` option.

- `-group` *groupname*—Display files owned by *groupname*.

- `-size` *n*—Display files of a given size represented by *n*. Follow the *n* value with a character to represent a unit of space. For example, `-size +10M` would display files that were 10 megabytes or larger.

You can change what the `find` command does when it finds a file. For example, the `-ls` option can provide detailed information about each file found:

```
[student@localhost ~]$ find /usr -name linux.words -ls 2> /dev/null
22096370 4840 -rw-r--r--  1 root     root      4953680 Jun  9  2014
➥/usr/share/dict/linux.words
```

Commonly used `find` options for specifying what to do with the files that are found:

- `-delete` Deletes the file.

- `-ls` Provides a long display listing of the files that were found (like the `ls -1` command).

- `-exec { } \;` Executes a command on that file that was found. For example:

  ```
  find /home/student -name sample.txt -exec more {} \;
  ```

> **Note**
>
> I know that the syntax here is very strange. In a nutshell, the `find` command generates a series of commands like this: `more file1; more file2; more file3`. The `{}` represents where to place the filename that was found and `\;` tells the `find` command "put a semicolon between each command to treat them as separate commands."

Comparing Files

As a developer, you are going to have different versions of files as you improve and bug-fix existing programs. This can cause confusion because determining whether two files are the same or somehow different is sometimes hard. In these cases, you should use the `cmp` and `diff` commands.

The `cmp` Command

If you only want to determine whether two files are different, not how they are different, then use the `cmp` command. Based on the output of the following commands, the `display.sh` and `show.sh` files contain identical content (this results in no output when `cmp` is executed) whereas `present.sh` contains different content:

```
[student@localhost ~]$ ls *.sh
display.sh  present.sh  show.sh
[student@localhost ~]$ cmp display.sh show.sh
[student@localhost ~]$ cmp display.sh present.sh
display.sh present.sh differ: byte 66, line 5
```

The `cmp` command is also useful for comparing two non-text files. For example, you could compare two files that contain compiled code.

The `diff` Command

If you want two see how two text files differ, use the `diff` command:

```
[student@localhost ~]$ diff display.sh present.sh
5c5
< if [-d /etc]
---
> if [ -d /etc ]
13a14,15
>
> echo "The end of the report"
```

The output of the `diff` command is essentially saying, "If you make these changes, then the files will look the same." Each section starts with a code that includes the line of the first file, what action to take and the line of the second file. For example, 5c5 means "Change line 5 of the first file to look like line 5 of the second file."

Additional lines after the "code" line indicate what the changes would look like:

```
< if [-d /etc]
---
> if [ -d /etc ]
```

The line that begins with < shows the current fifth line of the first file. The --- is just used to separate the lines, and the line that begins with the > shows the current fifth line of the second file.

Shell Features

The bash shell includes a large number of features designed to make it an easier and more powerful command-line environment. Some of these features, such as wildcards and redirection, have already been covered in Chapter 3.

In this section you learn about more bash shell features, including shell variables, aliases, and history. Knowing how to use these features will make it much easier to work in the bash shell and make you a more powerful software developer.

Shell Variables

Just like programming languages use variables to store values, the bash shell also stores critical shell information in variables. To create a variable, use the following syntax: VAR=value. To display a variable, use the echo command and place a $ character in front of the variable name:

```
[student@localhost ~]$ EDITOR=vi
[student@localhost ~]$ echo $EDITOR
vi
```

To display all variables, use the set command. There are many predefined variables, so you might want to pipe the output to the more or head command to limit the output. See Listing 4.3 for an example.

Listing 4.3   **The set command**

```
[student@localhost ~]$ set | head
ABRT_DEBUG_LOG=/dev/null
BASH=/bin/bash
BASHOPTS=checkwinsize:cmdhist:expand_aliases:extglob:extquote:force_
fignore:histappend:interactive_comments:login_shell:progcomp:promptvars:sourcepath
BASH_ALIASES=()
BASH_ARGC=()
BASH_ARGV=()
BASH_CMDS=()
BASH_COMPLETION_COMPAT_DIR=/etc/bash_completion.d
BASH_LINENO=()
BASH_REMATCH=()
```

Variables serve three primary purposes:

- **To store useful information for the user.** For example,

  ```
  DOCS=/usr/share/docs
  ```

- **To store useful information for the shell or a command.** For example, the EDITOR variable is used to tell commands like visudo and crontab which editor to use by default. For this to work, you must convert the variable to an environment variable (see the "Environment Variables" sidebar).

- **To store script data.** When creating bash shell scripts, you will need to store information. Variables are very useful for that purpose (see Chapter 8, "BASH Shell Scripting," for more details on BASH shell scripting).

Environment Variables

By default, variables are only available to the shell they are created in. However, you can tell the shell to pass variables to other commands by making them environment variables.

For example, if you want to pass the EDITOR variable to any command that is executed in the shell, execute the following commands:[5]

```
EDITOR=vi
export EDITOR
```

Aliases

If you find yourself using the find command daily to search the system for new shell scripts:

```
find / -name "*.sh" -ls
```

At some point you ask yourself, "Why do I need to type this long command every day?" The fact is, you don't need to. You can make an alias for this command, which can be much shorter and easier to type. For example:

```
alias myfind='find / -name "*.sh" -ls'
```

Now when you execute the myfind alias, it will run that long find command. However, you must create this alias every time you log in and every time you open a new shell. To have this happen automatically, place this alias command in a file named .bashrc in your home directory. You can also use this file to create variables that you want enabled every time you log in to the system.

History

Commands that you execute in a shell are saved in memory so you can execute them again. To see these commands, execute the history command (the output could be hundreds of commands, so limit the output with the tail command):

```
[student@localhost ~]$ history | tail -n 5
  258  alias hidden='ls -ld .*'
```

---

5 You can also do this in one step: export EDITOR=vi

```
259  alias c=clear
260  alias
261  date
262  history | tail -n 5
```

Each command is assigned a number. You can re-execute a command by using this number with an ! character preceding it:[6]

```
[student@localhost ~]$ !261
date
Sun May  1 01:06:21 PDT 2016
```

You can also bring up the previous command by pressing the up arrow key. This allows you to modify a command before re-executing it.

Permissions

Understanding file and directory permissions is critical for Linux developers because Linux is a multi-user environment and permissions are designed to protect your work from others. To understand permissions, you first need to know the types of permissions that are available in Linux and how these permissions differ when they are applied to files versus when they are applied to directories.

You also need to know how to set permissions. Linux provides two methods: the symbolic method and the octal (or numeric) method.

Viewing Permissions

To view the permissions of a file or directory, use the ls -l command:

```
[student@localhost ~]$ ls -l /etc/chrony.keys
-rw-r-----. 1 root chrony 62 May  9  2015 /etc/chrony.keys
```

The first ten characters of the output denote the file type (recall that - is for plain files and d is for directories) and the permissions for the file. Permissions are broken into three sets: the user owner of the file (root in the previous example), the group owner (chrony), and all other users (referred to as "others").

Each set has three possible permissions: read (symbolized by r), write (w), and execute (x). If the permission is set, the character that symbolizes the permission displays. Otherwise, a - character displays to indicate that permission isn't set. So, r-x means "read and execute are set, but write is not set."

---

6 The ! character is often called the bang character in Linux. Other common character nicknames include splat for * and hash for #.

Files versus Directories

What read, write, and execute permissions really mean depends on whether the object is a file or directory. For files, it means the following:

- **Read**—Can view or copy file contents.

- **Write**—Can modify file contents.

- **Execute**—Can run the file like a program; after you create a program, you must make it executable before you can run it.

For directories, it means the following:

- **Read**—Can list files in directory.

- **Write**—Can add and delete files in directory (requires execute).

- **Execute**—Can cd into directory or use in pathname.

The write permission on directories is potentially the most dangerous. If a user has write and execute permission on one of your directories, then that user can delete every file in that directory.

Changing Permissions

The chmod[7] command is used to change permissions on files. It can be used in two ways: symbolic method and octal method. With the octal method, the permissions are assigned numeric values:

- Read = 4

- Write = 2

- Execute = 1

With these numeric values, one number can be used to describe an entire permission set:

- 7 = rwx

- 6 = rw-

- 5 = r-x

- 4 = r--

- 3 = -wx

- 2 = -w-

- 1 = --x

- 0 = ---

---

7 Permissions used to be called *modes of access*, hence the origin of the name chmod (change mode of access).

So, to change the permissions of a file to `rwxr-xr--`, you execute the following command:

```
chmod 754 filename
```

With octal permissions, you should always provide three numbers, which will change all the permissions. But what if you only want to change a single permission of the set? For that, use the symbolic method by passing three values to the `chmod` command as shown in Table 4.1.

Table 4.1   **Symbolic method values**

Who	What	Permission
u = user owner	+	r
g = group owner	−	w
o = other	=	x
a = all sets		

The following demonstrates adding execute permission to all three sets (user owner, group owner, and others):

```
[student@localhost ~]$ ls -l display.sh
-rw-rw-r--. 1 student student 291 Apr 30 20:09 display.sh
[student@localhost ~]$ chmod a+x display.sh
[student@localhost ~]$ ls -l display.sh
-rwxrwxr-x. 1 student student 291 Apr 30 20:09 display.sh
```

Developer Tools

Knowing how to view files, modify file permissions, and use shell features are important for all Linux users. Developers also should know how to compress files and how to use the powerful filtering tool, the `grep` command.

File Compression Commands

As a developer you will be in a position to transfer files from one system to another. You might be downloading software from the Internet, uploading your programs to a server, or sending your programs to someone via email. In all of these cases, knowing how to merge files into a single file and compressing this merged file will be useful. This process makes transporting large amounts of data easy and quick as well as provides something that will take up less disk space.

Many commands in Linux enable you to create compressed files, including the `gzip`, `bzip2`, and `tar` commands.

The `gzip` Command

The purpose of the `gzip` command is to create a compressed version of a file. By default, it replaces the original file with the compressed version:

```
[student@localhost ~]$ cp /usr/share/dict/linux.words .
[student@localhost ~]$ ls -l linux.words
-rw-r--r--. 1 student student 4953680 May  1 09:19 linux.words
[student@localhost ~]$ gzip linux.words
[student@localhost ~]$ ls -l linux.words.gz
-rw-r--r--. 1 student student 1476083 May  1 09:19 linux.words.gz
```

If you want both the compressed and original file, you have to use the `-c` option to send the output to standard output and keep the original file. Of course, you don't really want the output to be sent to the screen, so redirect the compressed output to a file:

```
[student@localhost ~]$ ls -l linux.words
-rw-r--r--. 1 student student 4953680 May  1 09:19 linux.words
[student@localhost ~]$ gzip -c linux.words > linux.words.gz
[student@localhost ~]$ ls -l linux.words linux.words.gz
-rw-r--r--. 1 student student 4953680 May  1 09:19 linux.words
-rw-rw-r--. 1 student student 1476083 May  1 09:23 linux.words.gz
```

> **Note**
>
> Typically file extensions, such as .txt and .cvs, are unnecessary in Linux. However, they are important for files that you create with the `gzip` command. This utility expects the extension of .gz when it uncompresses a file. If you name the file linux.words.zipped, for example, the `gzip` command will attempt to use the file named linux.words.zipped.gz when uncompressing the file (and this will fail).

To uncompress a gzipped file, use the `-d` option:[8]

```
[student@localhost ~]$ ls -l linux.words.gz
-rw-rw-r--. 1 student student 1476083 May  1 09:23 linux.words.gz
[student@localhost ~]$ gzip -d linux.words.gz
[student@localhost ~]$ ls -l linux.words
-rw-rw-r--. 1 student student 4953680 May  1 09:23 linux.words
```

The `bzip2` Command

The difference between `gzip` and `bzip2` is how they perform the compression operation. In some cases, `gzip` results in better compression, whereas in others the `bzip2` command does. The `gzip` utility is the older of the two and considered more established, but the `bzip2` utility is used fairly often on modern Linux distributions.

---

8 You can also use the `gunzip` command.

Fortunately, the developers of bzip2 decided to use the same options that the gzip utility uses:

```
[student@localhost ~]$ ls -l linux.words
-rw-rw-r--. 1 student student 4953680 May  1 09:23 linux.words
[student@localhost ~]$ bzip2 linux.words
[student@localhost ~]$ ls -l linux.words.bz2
-rw-rw-r--. 1 student student 1711811 May  1 09:23 linux.words.bz2
[student@localhost ~]$ bzip2 -d linux.words.bz2
[student@localhost ~]$ ls -l linux.words
-rw-rw-r--. 1 student student 4953680 May  1 09:23 linux.words
```

Which One Should You Use?

Keep in mind that gzip and bzip2 are just two of the compression commands available on Linux. Others include the zip utility and the xz command. With so many to choose from, which should you use?

If you are only concerned about the compressed file being used on Linux, then it really comes down to compression ratio. Try them all, and find out which compresses the best (or the fastest because higher compression is often slower).

If you are considering compressing a file that will be used on other platforms, such as Microsoft Windows, I suggest using zip or gzip because they use a more standard compression algorithm.

The tar Command

The gzip and bzip commands are great for compressing a single file, but what if you want to merge a bunch of files together? Typically, this means using the tar[9] command.

To create a tar file (also called a **tar ball**), use the following syntax:

```
[student@localhost ~]$ tar -cvf zip.tar /usr/share/doc/zip-3.0
tar: Removing leading '/' from member names
/usr/share/doc/zip-3.0/
/usr/share/doc/zip-3.0/CHANGES
/usr/share/doc/zip-3.0/LICENSE
/usr/share/doc/zip-3.0/README
/usr/share/doc/zip-3.0/README.CR
/usr/share/doc/zip-3.0/TODO
/usr/share/doc/zip-3.0/WHATSNEW
/usr/share/doc/zip-3.0/WHERE
/usr/share/doc/zip-3.0/algorith.txt
```

You use the -c option to create the tar file. The -v option stands for *verbose* and results in a list of the files that are being merged into the tar file. You use the -f option to specify the name of the resulting tar file.[10]

---

9   The command comes from the phrase *Tape ARchive*. Or it could be *TApe aRchive*. You pick.

10 Note that for the tar command, the - character before the options is optional. So, tar cvf is the came as tar -cvf. A handful of Linux commands don't require the - character before options.

> **Note**
>
> What happens when you try to create a tar file and forget to provide a name for it? You get the following message:[11]
>
> ```
> tar: Cowardly refusing to create an empty archive
> ```

To list the contents of an existing tar file, use the -t option (t for *table of contents*:

```
[student@localhost ~]$ tar -tf zip.tar
usr/share/doc/zip-3.0/
usr/share/doc/zip-3.0/CHANGES
usr/share/doc/zip-3.0/LICENSE
usr/share/doc/zip-3.0/README
usr/share/doc/zip-3.0/README.CR
usr/share/doc/zip-3.0/TODO
usr/share/doc/zip-3.0/WHATSNEW
usr/share/doc/zip-3.0/WHERE
usr/share/doc/zip-3.0/algorith.txt
```

To extract the files from the tar ball, use the -x option:

```
[student@localhost ~]$ tar -xf zip.tar
```

In the current directory there should now be a usr directory with a directory structure of usr/share/doc/zip-3.0. All the extracted files are in the zip-3.0 directory.

By default, the tar command does not compress. However, you can have the tar command use either gzip or bzip2 to compress by using the -z (gzip) or -j (bzip2) options.

The grep Command

Many tools available on Linux are designed to perform operations on text data, but the most powerful and useful for a software developer is the grep command. This command is designed to act as a filter, only displaying the lines of data that match a pattern.

> **Origin of the Word** *grep*
>
> Clearly *grep* is not a real word. So, where did the name come from?
>
> It comes from a feature of the ed editor (an editor that predates the vi editor that you will learn about in Chapter 5). In the ed editor, you could display only the lines that contain a pattern by using the following syntax:
>
> ```
> :g/pattern/p
> ```
>
> Because the pattern could be a regular expression (regular expressions are covered in the next section), ed documentation typically displayed this command as
>
> ```
> :g/re/p
> ```
>
> The individual who created the grep command (Ken Thompson) also created the ed feature, so he naturally named the command after the feature.[12]

---

11 Okay, some Linux jokes are a little bit funny.

12 With this new Linux trivia, you are bound to be the life of any party.

For example, to view all the comment lines in a shell script, execute the following command:

```
[student@localhost ~]$ grep "#" /etc/rc.local
#!/bin/bash
# THIS FILE IS ADDED FOR COMPATIBILITY PURPOSES
#
# It is highly advisable to create own systemd services or udev rules
# to run scripts during boot instead of using this file.
#
# In contrast to previous versions due to parallel execution during boot
# this script will NOT be run after all other services.
#
# Please note that you must run 'chmod +x /etc/rc.d/rc.local' to ensure
# that this script will be executed during boot.
```

By default, the grep command matches the pattern regardless of whether it is part of another word. You can see the result of this by looking at line 2 of Listing 4.4 where the *the* is matched within the word *then*.

Listing 4.4 **Matching with grep**

```
[student@localhost ~]$ grep the /etc/bashrc | cat -n
     1 # will prevent the need for merging in future updates.
     2 if [ "$PS1" ]; then
     3   if [ -z "$PROMPT_COMMAND" ]; then
     4       if [ -e /etc/sysconfig/bash-prompt-xterm ]; then
     5       elif [ "${VTE_VERSION:-0}" -ge 3405 ]; then
     6       if [ -e /etc/sysconfig/bash-prompt-screen ]; then
     7   # if [ "$PS1" ]; then
     8 if ! shopt -q login_shell ; then # We're not a login shell
     9       # Need to redefine pathmunge, it gets undefined at the end
         ➥of /etc/profile
    10           if [ "$2" = "after" ] ; then
    11       if [ $UID -gt 199 ] && [ "'id -gn'" = "'id -un'" ]; then
    12       # and interactive - otherwise just process them to set envvars
    13         if [ -r "$i" ]; then
    14             if [ "$PS1" ]; then
```

If you only want to match a pattern as a separate word, use the -w option:

```
[student@localhost ~]$ grep -w the /etc/bashrc | cat -n
     1 # will prevent the need for merging in future updates.
     2       # Need to redefine pathmunge, it gets undefined at the end
         ➥of /etc/profile
```

Regular Expressions

Chapter 3 discussed wildcards, special characters that the bash shell uses to match filenames in a directory. Wildcards are fairly simple to use, because filenames are typically small and not very complex. However, text within a file can be much more rich and complex. To perform flexible matching with the `grep` command, use regular expressions (think "wildcards on steroids").

Regular expressions are a huge topic (seriously, enough to fill up a book larger than the size of this one). As a developer, you don't need to know everything about regular expressions, so to get you started, I just cover the basics.

As you can see from the following example, the `grep` command returns results regardless of where on the line the pattern is found:

```
[student@localhost ~]$ grep "growths" /usr/share/dict/linux.words
growths
ingrowths
outgrowths
regrowths
undergrowths
upgrowths
```

If you only want to see the lines that begin with the pattern, use the regular expression character ^ at the beginning of the pattern:

```
[student@localhost ~]$ grep "^growths" /usr/share/dict/linux.words
growths
```

If you only want to see the lines that end with the pattern, use the regular expression character $ at the end of the pattern.

Remember Listing 4.1?

Listing 4.1 is a bash shell script (with an error) that includes lines like the following:

```
ls -l /etc | grep "^d" | wc -l
ls -l /etc | grep "^-" | wc -l
ls -l /etc | grep "^l" | wc -l
```

These lines took the output of the `ls -l` command and sent it to the `grep` command to display file times. Lines from the `ls -l` command that begin with the letter *d* are directories. By sending this output to the `wc` command, you get a count of how many directories are in the /etc directory.

In Chapter 8, "BASH Shell Scripting," you will learn about the rest of what this bash shell script is doing.

Another useful regular expression character is the . character, which represents exactly one character. In the following example, `"r..t"` matches "root" on lines 1 and 2. For line 3 `"r..t"` matches "r/ft":

```
[student@localhost ~]$ grep "r..t" /etc/passwd | cat -n
     1    root:x:0:0:root:/root:/bin/bash
     2    operator:x:11:0:operator:/root:/sbin/nologin
     3    ftp:x:14:50:FTP User:/var/ftp:/sbin/nologin
```

Additional useful `grep` regular expressions (some of which require using the `-E` option for extended regular expressions) include

- `*` Matches zero or more of the previous character.
- `+` Matches one or more of the previous character (requires using the `-E` option).
- `.` Matches any single character.
- `[ ]` Matches a single character from a subset of characters; `[abc]` matches either an *a*, *b*, or *c*.
- `?` Matches an optional character; `a?` means "match either the character 'a' or nothing" (requires using the `-E` option).
- `|` Match one or another; `abc|xyz` matches either *abc* or *xyz* (requires using the `-e` option).
- `\` Escapes the special meaning of a regular expression character; `\*` matches simply a `*` character.

> **Note**
>
> Regular expressions are extremely useful, not just for the `grep` command, but many other Linux tools as well as many programming languages. This is a very good topic to expand your knowledge on to become a more powerful developer.

Searching for Files with `grep`

The `find` and `locate` commands are useful for finding files by name, but they can't find files based on the contents of a file. The `grep` command can search all files within a directory structure recursively if you use the `-r` option.

When you use the `grep` command in this manner, you probably want to use the `-l` option, which will list matching filenames (rather than listing every line in every file that matches). You probably also want to redirect STDERR to suppress error messages for files and directories that you don't have permission to. See Listing 4.5 for an example that searches for all bash shell scripts in the `/etc` directory structure.

Listing 4.5 **Searching with `grep`**

```
[student@localhost ~]$ grep -rl '^#!/bin/bash' /etc/* 2> /dev/null
/etc/auto.net
/etc/auto.smb
/etc/cron.daily/0yum-daily.cron
/etc/cron.daily/man-db.cron
/etc/cron.hourly/0yum-hourly.cron
/etc/init.d/netconsole
/etc/kernel/postinst.d/51-dracut-rescue-postinst.sh
```

```
/etc/NetworkManager/dispatcher.d/11-dhclient
/etc/NetworkManager/dispatcher.d/13-named
/etc/pki/tls/certs/renew-dummy-cert
/etc/ppp/ip-down
/etc/ppp/ip-up
/etc/ppp/ipv6-up
/etc/qemu-ga/fsfreeze-hook
/etc/rc.d/init.d/netconsole
/etc/rc.d/rc.local
/etc/rc.local
/etc/sysconfig/network-scripts/ifdown-eth
/etc/sysconfig/network-scripts/ifdown-tunnel
/etc/sysconfig/network-scripts/ifup-aliases
/etc/sysconfig/network-scripts/ifup-eth
/etc/sysconfig/network-scripts/ifup-sit
/etc/sysconfig/network-scripts/ifup-tunnel
/etc/sysconfig/network-scripts/ifup-wireless
/etc/sysconfig/network-scripts/ifdown-ib
/etc/sysconfig/network-scripts/ifup-ib
/etc/sysconfig/raid-check
/etc/vsftpd/vsftpd_conf_migrate.sh
/etc/X11/xinit/xinitrc.d/50-xinput.sh
/etc/X11/xinit/xinitrc.d/zz-liveinst.sh
/etc/X11/xinit/Xclients
/etc/X11/xinit/Xsession
```

Linux Humor

Who needs to go to the movies? Big screen Hollywood action is available right on your Linux computer. Type the following command, grab some popcorn, and enjoy:

```
telnet towel.blinkenlights.nl
```

P.S. To stop the "movie," hold down the Ctrl button and press the] key. Then type `quit` at the `telnet>` prompt and press the Enter key.

Summary

At this point you should have a solid foundation that will enable you to work in the Linux command-line environment. You learned the essentials, such as how to view a file and make use of bash shell features. You should now know how to secure your files using permissions. In the next chapter you will build on these tools to learn some important system administrative tasks of which developers should be aware.

5

Text Editors

As a developer, you will edit text files on a regular basis. This can sometimes pose a challenge because Linux offers a variety of editors. In many cases, you should be able to pick your editor, but sometimes you might be forced to use one of the standard editors, such as the vi editor.

This chapter focuses on the editors that are available on Linux distributions. The primary focus is on the vi (or vim) editor because it has the advantage of always being available on whatever Linux distribution you are working on. I introduce some additional editors to help you determine which tool will work best for your situation.

The vi Editor

Consider the early days of Unix, the precursor to Linux: A developer would sit down at a keyboard, ready to edit a program that he is working on. He stares at the printer (yes, printer, not monitor) considering what commands to execute. Monitors were very rare in the early 1970s and even if a developer had one, it was primarily designed to display the output of executed code, not to interactively edit files.

Instead, the developer would use a simple command-based editor, such as the ed editor. With this editor a developer could perform operations such as list the contents of a file (print the file), modify specific characters of a file, or save the contents of a file. However, he accomplished all this in a way that might seem foreign today. The developer wouldn't see what he was editing, but rather just assume the commands were successful (or print the file to verify).[1]

---

1 On some modern Linux distributions, the ed editor still exists. Try typing the command ed in a terminal window. If the editor does exist on your system, you will be placed in the ed editor environment (essentially a blank prompt). In reality, the only ed command you want to know is q because this quits the ed editor.

When monitors became more commonplace, the ed editor seemed like a clumsy way to edit a text file. In the mid-1970s a replacement editor named vi (short for visual) was introduced to Unix.[2] It was a great improvement over the ed editor[3] because you could actually see and move around in your document.

Why Learn vi?

You will soon discover that some editors are easier to use than vi. This discovery will result in your asking the question, "Why the heck should I bother learning the vi editor?" Several good reasons exist, even if you never plan on using the vi editor on a daily basis:

- **vi requires no GUI:** Many of the editing tools that this chapter introduces require a graphical user interface. Normally that is not a problem, but on many servers, the GUI isn't even installed because it tends to be a resource (CPU, memory, and hard drive space) hog. If you might be called upon to edit code on a server, then you might need to know a command-line editor like the vi editor.

- **vi is a very stable standard:** You could take a cryogenically frozen developer from the 1970s who used the vi editor, unfreeze him today and he could edit files using a modern vi editor. Certainly, features have been added to the vi editor since the 1970s, but the core functionality of vi does not change, making it very easy for you to use throughout your career without having to "relearn" how newer versions work.

- **vi is always there:** In every Linux distribution (and all Unix ones as well) the vi editor is there. After you know how to edit files with the vi editor, you can edit files on any Linux machine.[4]

- **Speed of use:** Although you might not believe this initially, you can actually edit files quickly using the vi editor. Granted, this will take many years of practice, but because you never need to use the mouse, you never need to take your hands off your keyboard when editing a file. The commands are also very short, so you can edit files very quickly.

What Is vim?

The vim editor[5] was released in 1991 as a clone of the vi editor. The vim editor has the same base functionality as the vi editor, but it has several additional features. Some of these features can be useful for software developers.

---

2 By the way, vi is pronounced *vee-eye*, not a single syllable *vi*.

3 Technically, it was an improvement of the ex editor, which was an improvement of the em editor, which as an improvement of the ed editor. Use this Unix trivia to entertain your friends at your next party. On second thought, maybe just keep this nugget to yourself.

4 Although removing the vi editor is possible, I've never heard of any distribution that has done so.

5 vim = a contraction of Vi IMproved

Your distribution might only have the vi editor. Many distributions have both the vi and vim editor. On some distributions, the command vi is actually a link to the vim editor.

An easy way to tell whether you are using the vi or vim editor is to try executing the vi command. If you are using vim, a message like the following appears: VIM – Vi IMproved. If you don't get this message, then you are using a standard vi editor.[6]

> **Note:**
> Unless stated otherwise, the commands shown in this chapter work in both the vi and vim editors. Any command that only works in vim is denoted as such.

Essential vi Commands

To become an expert vi user can take a lot of practice, but to be able to effectively edit files requires the knowledge of a subset of the large amount of vi commands.

It helps to have a large file to edit. All Linux distributions should come with a /etc/services file that is typically thousands of lines long. You can start by first copying this file to your home directory and then edit the copy with the vi command:

```
[student@fedora ~]$ cp /etc/services.
[student@fedora ~]$ vi services
```

Entering Insert Mode

When you first start the vi editor, you are placed in the command mode. This mode allows you to perform commands such as moving around the screen, copying text, and deleting text.

While in the command mode, you can't insert new text into your document because all the keyboard keys are assigned to command tasks. To insert new text, you must use the s command to move from command mode to insert mode. These commands include the following:

- i—New text will appear before the cursor position.
- a—New text will appear after the cursor position.
- I—New text will appear at the beginning of the line.
- A—New text will appear at the end of the line.
- o—Opens a new line below the line that contains the cursor; new text will be placed on this line.
- O—Opens a new line above the line that contains the cursor; new text will be placed on this line.

---

6 To exit vi/vim, type :q and then press the Enter key.

See Figure 5.1 for a visual description of how these vi commands work.

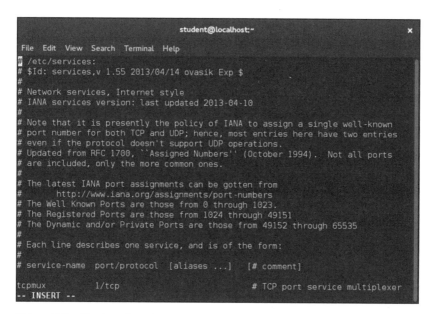

Figure 5.1   vi commands to enter insert mode

Note that when you are using the vim editor and enter the insert mode, the bottom part of the screen changes to indicate this. See the -- **INSERT** -- at the bottom of Figure 5.2.

Figure 5.2   The insert mode

If you are working in a standard vi editor, then -- **INSERT** -- does not appear at the bottom of the screen by default. To enable this feature in a standard vi editor, type the following command while in command mode:

`:set showmode`

When you want to return to command mode, just press the escape (Esc) key. This is normally denoted in documentation as <ESC>. If you return to the command mode, then the -- **INSERT** -- should disappear from the bottom of the screen.

Movement Commands

While in the command mode, you can move the cursor in your document by using a variety of keys. One of the common methods is to move the cursor one character to the left or right or one line up or down. You do this by using either the arrow keys on your keyboard or using the h, j, k, and l keys[7] as shown in Figure 5.3.

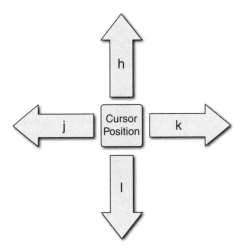

Figure 5.3   vi movement commands

Many additional movement commands are available, including the following:

- $ Move to the last column (character) on the current line
- 0   Move to the first column (character) on the current line
- w   Move to the beginning of the next word or punctuation mark
- W   Move to past the next space
- b   Move to the beginning of the previous word's punctuation mark
- B   Move to the beginning of the previous word, ignoring punctuation
- e   Move to the end of next word or punctuation mark
- E   Move to the end of next word, ignoring punctuation
-)   Move forward one sentence

---

7   Why use the h, j, k, and l keys when you can use the arrow keys? When the vi editor was developed, most keyboards didn't have arrow keys. Even today, rack-mounted servers are sometimes connected to dump terminals that have keyboards that lack arrow keys.

- (Move back one sentence

- } Move forward one paragraph

- { Move back one paragraph

- H Move to the top of the screen

- M Move to the middle of the screen

- L Move to the bottom of the screen

- [[Move to the beginning of the document

-]] Move to the end of the document

- G Move to the end of the document (same as]])

- xG Move to line x (you can also use :x)

Note that these are just some of the movement commands. Here's a suggestion: spend some time trying out these movement commands and then create a cheat sheet of the commands that you feel will be most useful to you. Make this a cheat sheet that you can add more commands to as you learn additional useful commands.[8]

Repeater Modifiers

In the previous section, you discovered that you can jump to a specific line in a document by typing a number followed by a G while you are in the command-mode. For example, the command 7G will take you to line number 7 in the document.

Placing a number before a command acts as a modifier. You can use modifiers on many different command-mode commands; for example:

- 3w Move forward three words

- 5i Insert something five times[9]

- 4(Move back three paragraphs

You can also use repeat modifiers on commands like deleting, copying, and pasting. Typically, if there is a command-mode command that you would logically want to execute multiple times, then repeat modifiers should work with that command.

---

8 Or visit the "Vi lovers" page (http://thomer.com/vi/vi.html) and download one of the reference cards under the "Vi pages/manuals/tutorials" section. Personally, I prefer to make my own because the commands that someone else finds useful, I might not find very helpful.

9 Be careful here. I once accidently typed the 8 key twice before pressing the i key to enter insert mode. After typing pages of text, I pressed the Esc key and received 88 times the text that I typed. Read on to learn how I fixed this problem quickly.

Are You Trying These Commands?

I had you copy the `/etc/services` file to your home directory so you can try the commands out. Remember, if you get stuck in insert mode, just press the Esc key to return to command mode.

Don't worry if you end up with a big mess in this file. It is just a practice file and you are about to learn how to correct mistakes.

Undoing

You can undo whatever change has been made to the document by typing the u character in command mode. In the standard `vi` editor, you can only undo a single action;[10] in fact, the u command acts as an undo/redo key.

If you are using the vim editor, you can undo several actions. Just keep pressing the u character to undo older modifications. You can perform a redo that undoes the changes performed by the undo command by using the `^r` (Ctrl+r) command.

Suppose you made a large number of changes since you opened the document and you want to discard them all. In this case, you probably want to close the document without saving and open it again. To close the document without saving changes, type the command `:q!`. You can find more on this command and other ways to quit the `vi` editor in the "Saving and Quitting" section later in this chapter.

Copying, Deleting, and Pasting

The following is a summary of commonly used copying commands. Keep in mind that you should execute these while in command mode:

- yw—Copy word. This actually copies from the current character in a word until the end of the word (including punctuation) and the white space after the word. So, if your cursor was on the *h* in "this is fun," the `cw` command would copy "his " into memory.

- yy—Copy current line.

- y$—Copy from current character to end of the line.

- yG—Copy current line to the end of the document.

You might be wondering "Why use the y character?" This is because the process of copying text into the memory buffer used to be called **yanking**.

---

10 Actually, if you don't move to another line, you can undo all changes on the current line by typing the u character while in command mode. However, I think you will find that you'll rarely use this feature because the moment you move to a new line, these undos are lost.

The following is a summary of commonly used deleting commands. Keep in mind, you should execute these while in command mode:[11]

- dw—Delete word; this command actually deletes from the current character in the word until the end of the word (including punctuation) and the white space after the word. So, if your cursor was on the *h* in "this is fun" the dw command would delete "his ", resulting in "tis fun."

- dd—Delete current line.

- d$—Delete from current character to end of the line.

- dG—Delete current line to the end of the document.[12]

- x—Delete the character the cursor is currently on (like a delete key).

- X—Delete the character before the character the cursor is currently on (like a backspace key).[13]

Where Are the Cut Commands?

When you use a delete command, the text that was deleted is placed into the copy buffer. As a result, no need exists for a separate set of cut commands.

Pasting commands can be a bit trickier because how they work depends on what you are pasting. For example, suppose you had copied a word into the buffer. In this case, the following describes how the paste commands would work:

- p—Pastes the buffer contents before the cursor

- P—Pastes the buffer contents after the cursor

The behavior is a bit different if you copy an entire line (or multiple lines) into the buffer:

- p—Pastes the buffer contents in the line above the cursor

- P—Pastes the buffer contents in the line below the cursor

---

11 Notice how similar these deleting commands are to the copying commands. Not only did this allow me to avoid a lot of extra typing in this book (call me lazy, or just an effective developer who "reuses" good "code"), but it highlights that most of the copying commands are just like deleting commands, which should make the process of learning them easier.

12 In a previous footnote, I mentioned that I once accidently inserted several pages of text 88 times. To fix this, I went to the first line in the second "set" and typed the dG command. This deleted all but the first copy of what I had typed with minimal effort.

13 If you are using the vim editor, you can use the delete key to delete the character you are currently on. However, the backspace key works like a back arrow key.

Finding Text

Finding text is a critical function for a software developer who is using the vi editor because error messages that appear when code is executed often include bits of code where the error occurs. You can search for text by using one of the following methods:

- /   While in command mode, type the / key; this character appears in the bottom-left corner of the terminal window. Now type what you want to search for and then press the Enter key. The vi editor will search *forward* in the document for the text you asked it to search for.

- ?   While in command mode, type the ? key; this character appears in the bottom-left corner of the terminal window. Now type what you want to search for and then press the Enter key. The vi editor will search *backward* in the document for the text you asked it to search for.

Suppose your search didn't find the specific match you were looking for. You can use the n command to find the next match. The n command searches forward when your last search started with the / key and searches backward when your last search started with the ? key.[14]

What if you searched for "/one" and realize you will need to press the n key many times to find what you are looking for? After furiously typing n repeatedly, you realize you went past the match that you wanted. To reverse the current search, use the N character (capital N rather than lowercase). When you're searching forward, N will reverse and search backward in the document. When you're searching backward, N will reverse and search forward in the document.

Case Sensitive

As with just about everything you use in Linux, the search function is case sensitive. In other words, a search of /the will not match the following line:

The end is near

Searching and Replacing

To search for text and replace it with other text, use the following format:

`:x,ys/pattern/replace/`

The values of x and y represent which lines you want to perform the search on. For example, to search and replace on only the first ten lines of the document, use the following syntax:

`:1,10s/I/we/`

---

14   Remember the regular expressions that were covered in the section on the grep command in Chapter 4? If not, go back and read that section again! Regular expressions show up in many tools in Linux, including the vi editor. For example, if you search for **^The**, the vi editor will only match lines that begin with *The*, rather than *The* anywhere on the line.

You can use the $ character to represent the last line in the document:

```
:300,$s/I/we/
```

So, to perform the substitution on the entire document, use the following:

```
:1,$s/I/we/
```

By default, only the first match on each line is replaced. Imagine if the line you are searching for and replacing looked like the following:

```
The dog ate the dog food from the dog bowl
```

If the command :s/dog/cat/ were executed on the previous line, then the result would be:

```
The cat ate the dog food from the dog bowl
```

To replace all occurrences on a line, add a g[15] at the end of the search command:

```
:s/dog/cat/g
```

Searching and replacing is case sensitive. Imagine if the line you are searching and replacing looked like the following:

```
The Dog ate the dog food from the dog bowl
```

If the command :s/dog/cat/ were executed on the previous line, then the result would be:

```
The Dog ate the cat food from the dog bowl
```

The result matched the second *dog* because the first one had a capital *D* character. To perform a case-insensitive search and replace, add an i at the end of the search command:

```
:s/dog/cat/i
```

Saving and Quitting

In the previous section, you typed a : character to perform a search and replace operation. Complex commands are performed in the **last line mode**, also called the **ex mode** in honor of the ex editor. The : character takes you to the bottom of the screen where the command appears as you type it.

Another operation you can do in this mode is save and quit your document:

```
:wq
```

> **Note**
>
> You must save before quitting, so you can't execute the command :qw because that will attempt to quit and then save.

---

15   You can think of g standing for *get them all*. It actually stands for *global*.

You might also want to just save, but continue working:

```
:w
```

You can also save to a different document, but there is a little gotcha to this operation that you will discover. Suppose you want to save changes made to your `services` file into a file called `myservices`. Execute the following:

```
:s myservices
```

The changes will be placed into this file. However, any further changes will be saved by default into the original services file. Most modern editors "switch" the default save document to whatever the last saved document was, but vi doesn't do this. To see your current document, type ^G (Ctrl+g).

So, if you want to edit the new file, you should quit the vi editor and open the new file.

If you make changes to a file and then try to quit without saving (`:q`), you receive an error message like the following:

```
E37: No write since last change (add ! to override)
```

To force quit (quit without saving changes), execute the following command:

```
:q!
```

Expanding Your vi Knowledge

Although the discussion has covered many vi commands, it really just scratches the surface. The vi editor is a very powerful tool with hundreds of commands. In addition, it provides some very advanced features, such as syntax highlighting, the capability to create macros, features for editing multiple files at the same time, and much more.

The vim editor has some very useful built-in documentation, but you must have a specific software package installed on Red Hat–based distributions[16] in order to be able to access this documentation. Chapter 6 covers installing software in greater detail. For now, just make sure you are logged in as the root user and execute the following command: `yum install vim-enhanced`

If this package is installed, you can execute the command `:help` while in the vim editor to see a help document. See Figure 5.4 for an example.

---

16 The help feature comes with vim by default on Debian-based distributions.

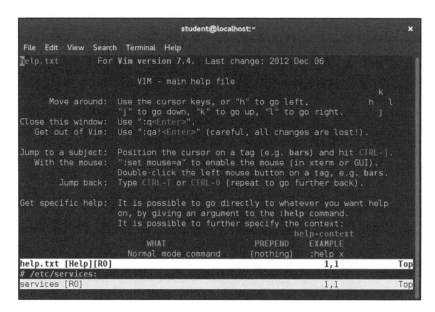

Figure 5.4   vim help output

Use your arrow keys (or h, j, k, and l) to scroll through the document. About 20 lines down, you will start to see some subtopics, as shown in Figure 5.5.

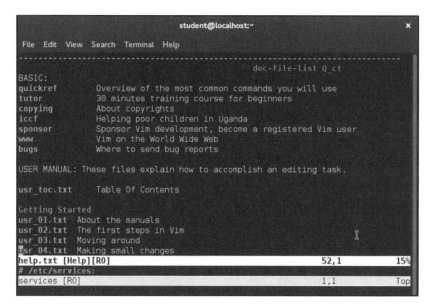

Figure 5.5   vim help topics

Each of these topics, such as quickref and usr_01.txt, are separate help topics. To view them, first exit from the current help document by typing the `:q` command. Then type a command like the following, replacing `topic` with the full name of the topic you want to view:

```
:help topic
```

For example, to see help on "Using syntax highlighting," type the following command:

```
:help usr_06.txt
```

vimtutor

A great tool to help you learn the vi editor is the `vimtutor` command. This command takes you into vi and provides a useful guide to learning the vim editor.

Additional Editors

A large number of editors are available that you can use in Linux. The focus of this section is to make you aware of these editors, not to teach you how to use them.

Note

It is likely that not all of these editors will be installed on your distribution. You might need to install additional software packages to have access to them.

Emacs

Like the vi editor, the Emacs editor was developed in the mid-1970s.[17] Linux users who like Emacs will praise how easy it is to use and how customizable it is. If you launch Emacs (just run the `emacs` command) while in a GUI-based terminal, it should open a GUI-based version of the program as shown in Figure 5.6. As you can see, the GUI-based version has menus in addition to the commands that you can execute via the keyboard.

---

17 Emacs versus vi/vim has been referred to as a "religious war" between the users of these editors. It is a war that I've always avoided; be aware that there are some in the Linux community who take this war very seriously.

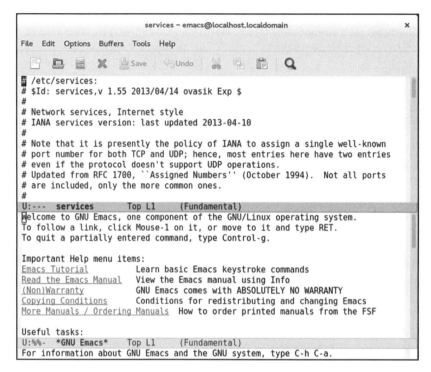

Figure 5.6   GUI-based Emacs

If you execute the Emacs editor in a command line–only environment, the editor will look like Figure 5.7.

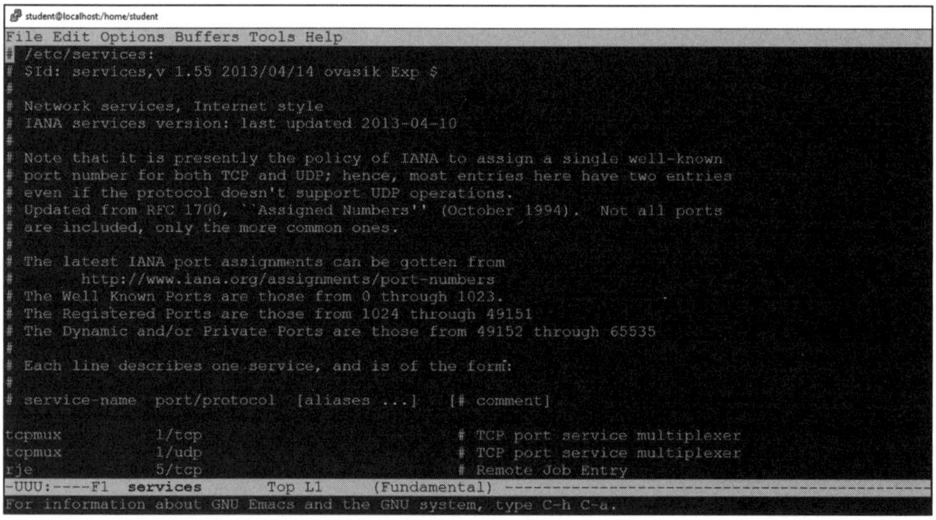

Figure 5.7   Text-based Emacs

> **GUI vim?**
>
> If you install the vim-X11 software package, you get access to a GUI-based version of the vim editor. Just execute gvim or vim -g on Red Hat–based distributions or vim-gtk on Debian-based distributions.

gedit and kwrite

These editors are fairly standard GUI-based editors (gedit comes with GNOME and kwrite comes with KDE). If you are used to Notepad on Microsoft Windows, then you will find these editors fairly easy to use (although somewhat limited).

The gedit editor typically is installed on distributions that use the GNOME desktop by default. The kwrite (or KATE) editor typically is installed on distributions that use the KDE desktop by default. However, you can easily install gedit on a system that uses KDE desktop or install kwrite on a GNOME desktop system.

nano and joe

The vi and emacs editors are extremely powerful. In some cases, you might find that you want to just use a simple edit in a command-line environment. The **gedit** and **kwrite** editors only work in GUI-based environments. The nano editor is also typically installed by default on most Linux distros.

The **nano** and **joe** editors provide a simple interface for editing text files. They are command line–only editors, so no GUI is required. See Figure 5.8 for an example of the nano editor.

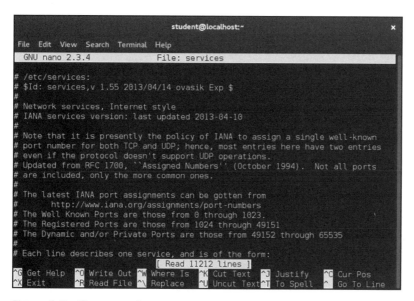

Figure 5.8   The nano editor

lime and bluefish

The **lime** and **bluefish** editors take the process of editing a text file to the next level by providing tools and features that are designed to help a developer create code. These tools provide features like syntax highlighting, insertion of code (by clicking a button), and automatic formatting (like automatically indenting code).

If you are going to make a career of coding on Linux, you should start to explore these tools (or many of the other similar editing tools). See Figure 5.9 for an example of the bluefish editor.

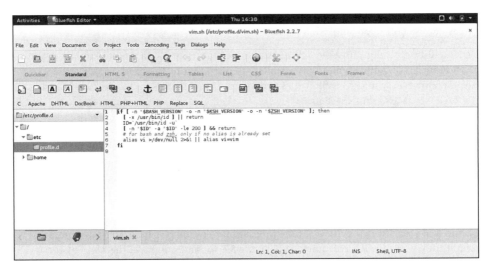

Figure 5.9   The bluefish editor

> ## Linux Humor
>
> Try this one in your shell:
>
>   bo@mintos:~ > cd /
>   bo@mintos:/ > touch me
>   touch: cannot touch 'me': Permission denied

Summary

The focus of this chapter was editors, primarily the vi or vim editor. We covered the basics of editing files in vi/vim, including how to start the editor, the three modes of operation, how to add and delete text, and some more advanced features. You were also introduced to some additional editors that are available in Linux. At this point, using these editors comes down to practice, which you should get plenty of when you start writing code on Linux.

System Administration

System administration is a huge topic that incorporates tasks such as configuring services, maintaining the health of the operating system, and keeping the system secure. Whole volumes have been devoted to teaching individuals how to administer a Linux distribution. As a developer, you should consider leaving the heavy lifting aspects of system administration to full-time system administrators.

However, that doesn't mean that you should never take on some of the responsibilities of system administration. Some tasks you will want to be able to accomplish without having to bother a system administrator. These tasks include installing software and maintaining user accounts. This chapter focuses on the essential system administration tasks that all software developers should have in their skill set.

Essential Tasks

In almost all cases, you should log in to the system using a regular user account and avoid logging in as the root user (the system administrator account). Routinely executing commands as the root user is just asking for trouble.

The root user has full control over the system, including the capability to delete all files and directories. The problem with working as the root user on a regular basis is that you can potentially damage your operating system, making it unusable. For example, consider the following command (but don't run this command!):

```
[root@fedora ~]$ rm -rf /
```

If you ran the preceding command while you were logged in as the root user, every file and directory on the system would be removed. As a regular user, this could result in loss of files in your home directory, but even that could be avoided by pressing Ctrl+C after you noticed all the error messages that would appear as you try to delete files that you don't have permission to delete.

So to summarize, the best practice is this: Log in as a regular user and only assume the identity of the root user if you need to perform a specific task as the root user.

Gaining Access to the Root Account

You can use three techniques to assume the identity of the root user:

- **Log in directly as the root user:** As previously mentioned, this is not the ideal method. Even system administrators avoid logging in directly as the root user.

- **Use the su command:** With the su command you can switch user to the root account if you know the root password. This command opens a new shell, and in that new shell you can commands as the root user. To return to your regular user account, you close the shell by executing the exit command.

- **Use the sudo command:** With the sudo command, you can execute commands as the root user without having to even know the root password. However, this feature does need to be set up by the system administrator to work properly.

Let's look at the su and sudo commands in a little more depth.

Using the su Command

To use the su command, execute the command as shown:

```
[student@localhost ~]$ id
uid=1000(student) gid=1000(student) groups=1000(student),10(wheel) context=unconfined_
u:unconfined_r:unconfined_t:s0-s0:c0.c1023
[student@localhost ~]$ su - root
Password:
[root@localhost ~]# id
uid=0(root) gid=0(root) groups=0(root) context=unconfined_u:unconfined_r:unconfined_
t:s0-s0:c0.c1023
```

Note that the id command displays your current user account. In this case the id command wasn't necessary because you can see the current user name in the prompt.

You will often see the argument root omitted when using the su command. If you don't specify a user account name, the root user is assumed by default:

```
[student@localhost ~]$ su -
Password:
[root@localhost ~]# id
uid=0(root) gid=0(root) groups=0(root) context=unconfined_u:unconfined_r:unconfined_
t:s0-s0:c0.c1023
```

The - option is not only strange because it lacks a character after the -, but it is also very important.[1] Without the - character, you will not fully switch to the root user account because the login scripts for the root user do not execute. The best way to demonstrate the difference between using the - and not using it is by looking at the code in Listing 6.1.

---

1 The - option is the same as the -l or -login options.

Listing 6.1   **The - option of the** `su` **command**

```
[student@localhost ~]$ su root
Password:
[root@localhost student]# pwd
/home/student
[root@localhost student]# echo $PATH
/usr/local/bin:/usr/bin:/usr/local/sbin:/usr/sbin:/home/student/.local/bin:/home/
student/bin
[root@localhost student]# exit
exit
[student@localhost ~]$ su - root
Password:
[root@localhost ~]# pwd
/root
[root@localhost ~]# echo $PATH
/usr/local/sbin:/usr/local/bin:/sbin:/bin:/usr/sbin:/usr/bin:/root/bin
```

Note that in Listing 6.1 when the - was not used, the current directory did not change and the value of the $PATH variable didn't change to the value for the root user. Using the - character fully switches you to the root account, the current directory switches to the root user's home directory, and the $PATH variable is set to the proper value for the root user (look at the end: /root/bin).

In many cases, it won't matter if you use the - character or not. However, sometimes not fully switching to the root user account can cause problems. The best practice is to use the - character when switching to the root account.

Important Note

Always remember that when you finish executing commands that require root privileges, switch back to your regular user account by executing the `exit` command.

Using the `sudo` Command

The `sudo` command allows you to execute commands as the root user without even knowing the root password but only if this feature has already been configured. On some distributions, notably Ubuntu and Mint, the `sudo` command is set up for the first user account by default:

```
bo@mintos:~ > sudo id
[sudo] password for bo:
uid=0(root) gid=0(root) groups=0(root)
```

Note that the password that was requested was not the root password, but rather the password of the current user (the bo user in this case). The `sudo` command takes another command as its argument and will execute that other command as the root user provided the correct password is provided and the `sudo` command has been set up correctly.

To set up the `sudo` command, add a line like the following in the `/etc/sudoers` file[2]:

```
bo      ALL=(ALL:ALL) ALL
```

The previous line would allow the user bo to use the `sudo` command to execute commands as the root user. Note that you can also apply this feature to entire groups[3] as shown in the following:

```
bo@mintos:~ > sudo grep %sudo /etc/sudoers
%sudo  ALL=(ALL:ALL) ALL
bo@mintos:~ > id
uid=1000(bo) gid=1000(bo) groups=1000(bo),4(adm),24(cdrom),27(sudo),30(dip),
46(plugdev),108(lpadmin),111(sambashare)
```

So, the reason why the bo user in the previous example can execute commands as the root user using the `sudo` command is because the bo user is a member of the sudo group.

If you need to give `sudo` access to a user or group, first switch to the root account and then execute the `visudo` command. This command automatically edits the `/etc/sudoers` file using the `vi` or `vim` editor. One advantage of using the `visudo` command rather than the regular `vi` or `vim` editor is that the `visudo` command performs some basic error checking when you save your changes.

Displaying Disk Usage

As a developer, displaying disk usage can be an important task. The amount of free space available will have an impact regarding what software you can install on the system. In addition, the programs you create might be very large or create large files, so displaying disk usage can be critical to making sure enough room exists for your program data.

On a Linux system, the space on the hard drive is broken into chunks called partitions or volumes. This is also true on other operating systems, such as Microsoft Windows; however, typically the result is a bit different. Making a partition out of an entire hard disk is common practice on Windows OS, whereas in Linux creating several partitions (or volumes[4]) on one hard disk is common.

---

2   Note that this is a very simple example and perfectly fine for a standalone system. However, for a system in which security is a concern, you should learn more about the `sudo` command or have a system administrator set up this feature.

3   A group in Linux is a collection of user accounts. Managing groups is covered in detail later in this chapter.

4   The difference between a partition and a volume is not critical for developers to understand. If you choose to become a system administrator, the difference becomes very important because they are managed differently. Because this book is for developers, I have chosen not to describe these differences. Consider them both to be a container where files and directories can be stored.

To display these partitions, including how much space is available, execute the `df` command as shown in the following:[5]

```
[student@localhost ~]$ df -h
Filesystem               Size  Used Avail Use% Mounted on
/dev/mapper/centos-root  6.7G  4.1G  2.6G  61% /
devtmpfs                 1.9G     0  1.9G   0% /dev
tmpfs                    1.9G   88K  1.9G   1% /dev/shm
tmpfs                    1.9G   17M  1.9G   1% /run
tmpfs                    1.9G     0  1.9G   0% /sys/fs/cgroup
/dev/sda1                497M  196M  302M  40% /boot
tmpfs                    389M  8.0K  389M   1% /run/user/0
```

The `Filesystem` column is used to indicate the partition (/dev/sda1) or volume (/dev/mapper/centos-root). Lines that don't represent a path to a file, such as devtmpfs or tmpfs, are memory-based filesystems and are not important for this topic.

The `Mounted on` column indicates to which directory structure the partition or volume is attached. Recall that, unlike Microsoft Windows, devices are not assigned drive letters but rather are placed under directory structures, like the `/boot` directory.

Based on the output of the `df` command, you can see how much space is available. For example, in the previous output, the `/boot` directory structure could support up to 302MB more data. The following directory structures are normally the most critical for developers to be aware of the available space:

- `/usr`—Location where new software will be installed

- `/home`—Home directories for regular users, including your own account

- `/tmp`—A location to store temporary files. As a developer you might need to create a file to hold data while your program is executing. Placing this file in the home directory of the user who is running the program is not ideal (they might delete it accidently). The `/tmp` directory is the best place to store such a file.

> **Note**
>
> If you don't see `/usr`, `/home`, or `/tmp` in the `Mounted on` column of the output of the `df` command, then these directories are not separate partitions or volumes, but rather are part of the `/` directory structure.

Determining how much space the files in a specific directory use on the hard disk is also useful. This can be important when you want to see how much space the removal of some large files within a directory can free up. To see how much space the files in a directory (and all subdirectories) are using, use the `du` command:

```
[student@localhost ~]$ du -sh /usr/sbin
54M    /usr/sbin
```

---

5 Use the `-h` option to show the output in human-readable sizes rather than one kilobyte block sizes.

The -s option displays a summary of the entire base directory, rather than each separate subdirectory. The -h option shows human-readable sizes.

Managing Software

Most of what appears in this book works the same (or at least similarly) on different distributions. Software management is different, because three different sets of tools are available to enable you to add and remove software. Which set of tools you use depends on the distribution on which you are working:

- yum and rpm—These tools enable you to manage software on Red Hat Enterprise Linux, CentOS, Fedora, and other Red Hat–based distributions.

- apt-get and dpkg—These tools enable you to manage software on Debian, Ubuntu, Mint, and other Debian-based distributions.

- zypper and rpm—These tools enable you to manage software on SUSE and SUSE-based distributions.

The rpm and dpkg commands perform very similar tasks. Historically, they were designed to install software packages that had been downloaded to the local system. This function is now normally handled by the yum, apt-get, and zypper commands, which are used to both download the package and install it. These commands download the package from a server called a repository.

The advantage of the yum, apt-get and zypper commands over the rpm and dpkg commands is that package dependencies are automatically taken care of. So, if a package needs three other packages to work successfully, the yum, apt-get, and zypper commands would also download and install these packages.

You can also use all of these commands to remove software packages. Again, the yum, apt-get, and zypper commands have an advantage over the rpm and dpkg commands because they check dependency issues before removing the package. So, if you try to remove a package that is required by another package, an error message appears.

So why would you ever use the rpm or dpkg commands? The yum, apt-get, and zypper commands are really front-end programs that eventually run rpm and dpkg commands. The rpm and dpkg commands have some more powerful options that can't be accessed by the yum, apt-get, or zypper commands, particularly options regarding querying information regarding packages. This is much more critical for system administrators than it is for developers, so you will likely run the yum, apt-get, and zypper commands much more often than rpm or dpkg.

Developers often install new software packages to enhance what features (or programming languages) they can use on the system. Keep in mind that installing and removing software requires root privileges.

Listing and Finding Software

Sometimes one of the challenges to installing software is trying to find the correct name for the software package. On Red Hat–based systems, you can execute the yum search command to query the repository for packages that match a word or pattern:

```
[root@localhost ~]# yum search editor | head
Loaded plugins: fastestmirror, langpacks
Loading mirror speeds from cached hostfile
 * base: centos.mia.host-engine.com
 * epel: linux.mirrors.es.net
 * extras: mirrors.sonic.net
 * updates: mirror.steadfast.net
========================= N/S matched: editor =========================
ckeditor.noarch : WYSIWYG text editor to be used inside web pages
ckeditor-samples.noarch : Sample files for ckeditor
dconf-editor.x86_64 : Configuration editor for dconf
```

The yum search command can produce a lot of output, so consider using the grep command to perform a secondary filter:

```
[root@localhost ~]# yum search editor | grep GUI
nedit.x86_64 : A GUI text editor for systems with X
root-guibuilder.x86_64 : GUI editor library for ROOT
torrent-file-editor.x86_64 : Qt based GUI tool designed to create and edit
```

To search for a package on a Debian-based system, use the apt-get search *term* command (replace *term* with your search term). To install a package on a SUSE-based system, use the zypper search -t *term* command.

To list currently installed packages on Red Hat–based systems, use the yum list installed command:

```
[root@localhost ~]# yum list installed | tail
yelp-libs.x86_64                  1:3.14.2-1.el7              @base
yelp-xsl.noarch                   3.14.0-1.el7               @base
yum.noarch                        3.4.3-132.el7.centos.0.1   @base
yum-langpacks.noarch              0.4.2-4.el7                @base
yum-metadata-parser.x86_64        1.1.4-10.el7               @anaconda
yum-plugin-fastestmirror.noarch   1.1.31-34.el7              @base
yum-utils.noarch                  1.1.31-34.el7              @base
zenity.x86_64                     3.8.0-5.el7                @base
zip.x86_64                        3.0-10.el7                 @anaconda
zlib.x86_64                       1.2.7-15.el7               @base
```

The yum list installed command also produces a lot of output. Consider piping the output to the more or grep command. Note that the first column of the output of this command displays the package name, the second column displays the version of the package, and the third column displays the repository name where the package was installed from.

To list all installed packages on a Debian-based system, use the `dpkg -l` command. To list all installed packages on a Red Hat–based system, use the `rpm -qa` command.

Installing Software

On Red Hat–based systems, install a package using the `yum install` command as shown in Listing 6.2.

Listing 6.2 **The `yum install` command**

```
[student@localhost Desktop]$ su -
Password:
[root@localhost ~]# yum install kernel-doc
Loaded plugins: fastestmirror, langpacks
Loading mirror speeds from cached hostfile
 * base: centos.mia.host-engine.com
 * epel: linux.mirrors.es.net
 * extras: mirrors.sonic.net
 * updates: mirror.steadfast.net
Resolving Dependencies
--> Running transaction check
---> Package kernel-doc.noarch 0:3.10.0-327.28.2.el7 will be installed
--> Finished Dependency Resolution

Dependencies Resolved

================================================================================
 Package          Arch         Version              Repository       Size
================================================================================
Installing:
 kernel-doc       noarch       3.10.0-327.28.2.el7  updates          13 M
Transaction Summary
================================================================================
Install  1 Package
Total download size: 13 M
Installed size: 48 M
Is this ok [y/d/N]: y
Downloading packages:
kernel-doc-3.10.0-327.28.2.el7.noarch.rpm                  |  13 MB   00:03
Running transaction check
Running transaction test
Transaction test succeeded
Running transaction
  Installing : kernel-doc-3.10.0-327.28.2.el7.noarch                     1/1
  Verifying  : kernel-doc-3.10.0-327.28.2.el7.noarch                     1/1
Installed:
  kernel-doc.noarch 0:3.10.0-327.28.2.el7
Complete!
```

To install a package on a Debian-based system, use the `apt-get install` command. To install a package on a SUSE-based system, use the `zypper install` command.

Removing Packages

Although developers often want to install packages on their own systems, wanting to remove or perform more advanced package manipulation commands is not as common. The `rpm` and `dpkg` commands were mentioned in the event you want to learn more about package management, but this is normally something that interests system administrators more.

In the event you do want to remove a software package, switch to the root account and run the proper command for your distribution:[6]

```
yum remove package_name

apt-get remove package_name or apt-get purge package_name

zypper remove package_name
```

User Accounts

Typically, maintaining user accounts is the responsibility of the system administrator. However, this can also be an important task for a software developer because you might want to be able to test your software using different user accounts. For example, you might want to have different accounts to test access for unprivileged users to a database.

This section focuses on the basics of creating, modifying, and deleting user accounts, and also explores the topic of group accounts.

Adding User Accounts

To add a user account, you need root privileges. GUI-based tools are available that you can use to create user accounts. However, they differ between distributions. The command-line tools are easy enough and you can use them to quickly create user accounts.

To create a user account, execute the `useradd` command as shown in the following:

```
[root@localhost ~]# useradd julia
[root@localhost ~]# tail -1 /etc/passwd
julia:x:1001:1001::/home/julia:/bin/bash
[root@localhost ~]# ls /home
julia   student
```

Notice the new entry in the /etc/password file, one of the files that contains user account information. To see details about the format of this file, execute the `man 5 passwd` command.

---

6 The `purge` argument to `apt-get` removes the package entirely. The `remove` argument removes everything except the configuration files (left behind in case you reinstall the software at a later date).

The new user was provided with a home directory automatically (/home/julia). This does not happen on all distributions; on some distros you must specify the name of the home directory with the -d option and tell the useradd command to create this home directory with the -m option:

```
[root@localhost ~]# useradd -d /home/julia -m julia
```

Typically the default settings for the user account are fine for accounts that you are creating for testing purposes. A few settings that you might want to modify include the following:

- -s Specify the login shell. For example: -s /bin/tcsh
- -g Specify the primary group for the account. For example: -g sudo
- -G Specify the primary group(s) for the account. For example: -G sudo,payroll

After creating the user account, assign the new account with a password by executing the passwd command as shown in the following:

```
[root@localhost ~]# passwd julia
Changing password for user julia.
New password:
Retype new password:
passwd: all authentication tokens updated successfully.
```

Bad Passwords

You might get a warning message like the following when assigning a password to a user account:

```
BAD PASSWORD: The password fails the dictionary check - it is based on a
dictionary word
```

If the system you are working on has access to the Internet, you should heed this warning and use a more complex password. However, if this is an internal-only system, making a more complex password can be more trouble than it is worth.

Ask yourself, "Will I ever connect this system to the Internet?" If the answer is "yes," make a more complex password.

Modifying User Accounts

To change a user account, use the usermod command. The usermod command accepts the same options as the useradd command. So, to change the login shell for a user, use the -s option as shown in the following:

```
[root@localhost ~]# grep julia /etc/passwd
julia:x:1001:1001::/home/julia:/bin/bash
[root@localhost ~]# usermod -s /bin/tcsh julia
[root@localhost ~]# grep julia /etc/passwd
julia:x:1001:1001::/home/julia:/bin/tcsh
```

If you look at the last field of data in the "julia" line of the /etc/passwd file, you can see that the login shell has changed from /bin/bash to /bin/tcsh.

Deleting User Accounts

To delete a user account, use the `userdel` command. If you want to delete both the account and the user's home directory, use the `-r` option. Not using the `-r` option removes the account from the `/etc/passwd` file (and other files that contain user account information), but does not remove the user's home directory and its contents.

```
[root@localhost ~]# userdel -r julia
```

Understanding Groups

Chapter 4, "Essential Commands" mentioned group accounts during the discussion on permissions. To understand how important group membership is, consider the output of the following commands:

```
[root@localhost ~]# id sarah
uid=1002(sarah) gid=1002(sarah) groups=1002(sarah)
[root@localhost ~]# ls -l /tmp/sample.txt
-rw-r-----. 1 root wheel 158 Aug 16 21:11 /tmp/sample.txt
```

Based on the output of the previous `id` command, you can see that the user sarah is a member of one group (the group named sarah). If you look at the output of the previous `ls -l` command, you can see that the `/tmp/sample.txt` file is owned by the user root and the wheel group. So, in this situation, the permissions for the user sarah are `---`, the "others" section of permissions.

What if the root user wanted the user sarah to be able to view this file? By adding the user sarah to the wheel group, she would have the permissions `r--`, allowing her to view the contents of the file:

```
[root@localhost ~]# usermod -aG wheel sarah
[root@localhost ~]# id sarah
uid=1002(sarah) gid=1002(sarah) groups=1002(sarah),10(wheel)
[root@localhost ~]# ls -l /tmp/sample.txt
-rw-r-----. 1 root wheel 158 Aug 16 21:11 /tmp/sample.txt
```

Managing Groups

To create a new group, use the `groupadd` command:

```
[root@localhost ~]# groupadd staff
```

To add a user to a group, use the `-G` option to the `usermod` command. *Very important*: Make sure you use the `-a` option with the `-G` option. Using `-G` alone removes the user from all of their secondary groups. See the following for the wrong way to do this:

```
[root@localhost ~]# id sarah
uid=1002(sarah) gid=1002(sarah) groups=1002(sarah),10(wheel)
[root@localhost ~]# usermod -G staff sarah
[root@localhost ~]# id sarah
uid=1002(sarah) gid=1002(sarah) groups=1002(sarah),1003(staff)
```

Notice the output of the previous `id` commands. You can see that the `usermod` command removed the user sarah from the wheel group. The following demonstrates the right way to add a user to a group:

```
[root@localhost ~]# id sarah
uid=1002(sarah) gid=1002(sarah) groups=1002(sarah),10(wheel)
[root@localhost ~]# usermod -a -G staff sarah
[root@localhost ~]# id sarah
uid=1002(sarah) gid=1002(sarah) groups=1002(sarah),10(wheel),1003(staff)
```

To remove a group, you might want to first use the `find` command to search the filesystem for all files owned by that group:

```
[root@localhost ~]# find / -group staff -ls 2> /dev/null
27304379    4 -rw-r-----  1 root   staff    158 Aug 16 21:11 /tmp/sample.txt
```

This is an important step because you should change the group ownership of these files to another group before removing the group. After you change the group ownership, you can use the `groupdel` command to delete the group:

```
[root@localhost ~]# chgrp wheel /tmp/sample.txt
[root@localhost ~]# ls -l /tmp/sample.txt
-rw-r-----. 1 root wheel 158 Aug 16 21:11 /tmp/sample.txt
[root@localhost ~]# groupdel staff
```

Linux Humor

If you are like me (or 99% of folks who work in Linux), you will eventually end up typing the command `sl` instead of the `ls` command. Why not make the result a bit more interesting than `bash: sl: command not found...`?

First, install the package named `sl` (choose the right command for your distribution):

```
yum install sl

apt-get install sl

zypper install sl
```

Now, type `sl` and press the Enter key!

Summary

A system administrator performs many additional tasks that were not covered in this chapter. However, the chapter did cover the administrative tasks that you, as a software developer, might routinely perform. You should now know to switch to the root account to perform system administration tasks. You also learned how to display disk usage, add and remove software, and manage group and user accounts.

III

Linux Programming Languages

One of the more important benefits to Linux is the vast amount of software that is freely available for the operating system. This poses both advantages and disadvantages. For example, having dozens of text editors to choose from is an advantage because that means you aren't "locked into" using an editor that you really don't like. However, it can also be a disadvantage because exploring the different editors to find one that suits you best might take some time.

The same can be said for programming languages. Many languages are available, and finding the one that best fits your programming style often takes a lot of trial and error. The focus of this part of the book is to provide a review of some of the more popular languages that are available for Linux. Chapter 7 provides general information about these languages and Chapters 8 through 11 provide additional details about select languages.

Overview of Linux Programming Languages

Most Linux programming languages[1] can be placed into two general categories: scripting languages (sometimes called **interpreted** languages) and compiled languages (sometimes called **structured** languages). There isn't a strict definition that separates these categories, but the following provides the essential differences:

- Complied languages cannot be executed directly from source code. The source code must be converted into compiled code first.

- Scripts traditionally are not compiled.

- Scripting languages are typically easier to learn.

- Scripts typically take less coding to perform a task.

As an example of how these categories are not strictly defined, consider this: Perl is a popular scripting language that is executed directly from source code, but before executing it is compiled into memory and the compiled form of the code is executed.

Scripting Languages

Many scripting languages are available for Linux, making it difficult to create a complete list in this book. However, you should find that the languages described in this section are the most popular and widely used on Linux distributions.

---

1 Although I refer to these languages as "Linux programming languages," be aware that most of these languages could also be available on other platforms, including Microsoft Windows.

BASH Shell Scripting

In Chapters 2–6 you learned the basics of working in Linux and the BASH shell.[2] You can also use those commands you learned in shell scripting programs. For example, suppose you routinely execute the following commands:

```
cd /home
ls -l /home > /root/homedirs
du -s /home/* >> /root/homedirs
date >> /root/homedirs
```

Instead of executing each of these commands manually, day after day, you can place all the commands into a file, make the file executable, and then run the file as a program:

```
[root@fedora ~]$ more /root/checkhome.sh
#!/bin/bash

cd /home
ls -l /home > /root/homedirs
du -s /home/* >> /root/homedirs
date >> /root/homedirs
[root@fedora ~]$ chmod a+x /root/checkhome.sh
[root@fedora ~]$ /root/checkhome.sh
```

Because you can use Linux commands natively in BASH shell scripts, this scripting language can be extremely powerful. Another advantage of using this language is that you can be confident that just about every Linux (and UNIX) distribution will have the BASH shell, making it easy to port a script from one system to another.

In addition to being able to use Linux commands in BASH shell scripts, you should be aware that this language has other programming features, such as:

- Variables
- Loop controls (if, while, and so on)
- Exit status values
- The ability to source code from other files

With all of its advantages, BASH shell scripting has some disadvantages, including:

- It lacks some advanced programming features, such as object-oriented programming.
- It is often much slower than executing other languages as each command is normally executed as a separate process.[3]

---

2 Given that BASH stands for Bourne-Again SHell, it is actually redundant to refer to the scripting component of BASH as "BASH shell scripting." However, just as the term ATM machine (ATM=Automated Teller Machine) has become standard, the term BASH shell scripting has become standard.

3 This isn't always the case as some commands are built-in shell commands that don't require a separate process.

Even with these disadvantages, BASH shell scripting is very popular in Linux. In fact, a search for BASH scripts (files that end in .sh) on a typical Linux distribution normally yields hundreds of results:

```
[root@fedora ~]$ find / -name "*.sh" | wc -l
578
```

Because of this, Chapter 8, "BASH Shell Scripting," is devoted to additional details regarding BASH shell scripting.

Perl Scripting

In the mid-1980s, a developer named Larry Wall began work on a new scripting language that would eventually be named Perl. At the time he was working on UNIX-based systems, which had tools such as the C programming language, the Bourne Shell scripting language (precursor to BASH), and `sed` and `awk` (more about these tools later). However, none of these tools worked as he wanted them to, so he created his own language.

Of course, Larry didn't want to lose the features that he did like about these tools, so he combined the features that he liked into his new language. This resulted in a language that looks a bit like C, a bit like shell scripting, and a bit like a hodgepodge collection of UNIX utilities.

Which Scripting Language Is the Best?

I believe trying to list the pros and cons of each scripting language is a mistake. To begin with, this is often a matter of opinion.[4] For example, Perl is a very flexible language whereas Python (see the next section) is more structured. If I want to write a quick script and I am not worried about maintaining the code long term, then flexibility might be a pro and structure a con. However, if I was working with multiple developers on a larger product, then structure might be a pro and flexibility a con.

Rather than trying to compare and contrast the pros and cons of each scripting language, I try to focus on what developers typically like about each language and what each language is typically used for. I would rather you decide what aspect of a language is a feature versus a liability.

Several aspects of Perl that developers like include the following:

- You can very quickly write Perl code because much of what you need for basic scripting is already built into the core language.

- Perl code is very flexible; you are not limited by the structure as much as some other languages.

- Perl's syntax is fairly simple, derived primarily from the C language.

---

4 Warning: Discussions on this matter often escalate to the level of a serious "religious war."

- It normally doesn't take very long to learn Perl.

- Perl has very powerful features, such as robust regular expressions.

Although Perl can be used for many different applications, it is often used for the following:

- **Data parsing**—Perl has powerful regular expression features that make it ideal for data munging (pulling chunks from data and generating reports).

- **Web development**—Perl is often a component of LAMP-based[5] technology because of its web development features, including Common Gateway Interface (CGI).

- **Code testing**—Because Perl is easy and quick to code, developers often use it to create tools to test their applications.

- **GUI programs**—Additional Perl modules (libraries), such as WxPerl and Tk, provide Perl programmers with the option of easily creating a GUI-interface for users to interact with the Perl code.

- **Administrative tools**—System administrators create Perl scripts to help them automate administrative tasks.

Chapter 9, "Perl Scripting," provides additional details regarding the creation of Perl programs.

Python Scripting

The beginnings of Python are best described by Guido van Rossum, its creator, who wrote the following as a forward for a book on Python published in 1996:

> Over six years ago, in December 1989, I was looking for a "hobby" programming project that would keep me occupied during the week around Christmas.
> My office ... would be closed, but I had a home computer, and not much else on my hands. I decided to write an interpreter for the new scripting language I had been thinking about lately: a descendant of ABC that would appeal to Unix/C hackers.
> I chose Python as a working title for the project, being in a slightly irreverent mood (and a big fan of Monty Python's Flying Circus).

Little did he know that Python would one day become one of the world's most popular scripting languages. Since that fateful Christmas break in the late 1980s, Python has developed over time into a robust programming language that is the core of many Linux tools and open source projects.

---

5   LAMP = Linux, Apache HTTP Server, MySQL, and Perl (or PHP). LAMP is a collection of technologies that make up a solution stack to provide web services.

One of the driving philosophies of Python is well-structured code. Python enforces this with rules such as a very rigid indentation scheme. You can see how seriously Python developers take the concept of well-structured code by reading some of the rules defined by the document "Zen of Python":

- Beautiful is better than ugly.
- Explicit is better than implicit.
- Simple is better than complex.
- Complex is better than complicated.
- Flat is better than nested.
- Sparse is better than dense.
- Readability counts.

In addition to being a well-structured language, the following components make Python a popular language:

- It has object-oriented features.
- It has a large standard library.
- It is extendable or embedded.
- The data structures provided by Python are more diverse than those of many languages.

Although Python can be used for many different applications, it is often used for the following:

- **Network-based applications**—By using Twisted, a Python-based network framework, network-based applications can be developed.
- **Web development**—The Apache Web Server provides the option of using Python scripts for dynamic websites.
- **Scientific applications**—Several libraries are available for Python that make it a good choice to create scientific applications.
- **System tools**—Linux developers often use Python to create system tools for the operating system.

Additional details regarding the creation of Python programs are provided in Chapter 10, "Python Scripting."

Additional Scripting Languages

Although this book focuses on BASH shell, Perl, and Python scripting, other scripting languages exist that you might want to explore when considering a Linux scripting language.

Ruby

Developed in the mid-1990s by Yukihiro Matsumoto, Ruby's origin is best described by its creator:

> I was talking with my colleague about the possibility of an object-oriented scripting language. I knew Perl (Perl4, not Perl5), but I didn't like it really, because it had the smell of a toy language (it still has). The object-oriented language seemed very promising. I knew Python then. But I didn't like it, because I didn't think it was a true object-oriented language—OO features appeared to be add-on to the language. As a language maniac and OO fan for 15 years, I really wanted a genuine object-oriented, easy-to-use scripting language. I looked for but couldn't find one. So I decided to make it.[6]

Initially Ruby wasn't as popular as Perl and Python, although it was praised for being a good object-oriented scripting language. Ruby became more popular when Ruby on Rails, a web application framework, was introduced.

Ruby Essentials

Is it installed?

```
root@centos:~# which ruby
/usr/bin/ruby
```

Install (if needed):

- Red Hat/Fedora/CentOS: `yum install ruby`
- Debian/Mint/Ubuntu: `apt-get install ruby`

Sample script:

```
root@centos:~# more hello.rb
#!/usr/bin/ruby
puts "Hello World"
root@centos:~# chmod a+x hello.rb
root@centos:~# ./hello.rb
Hello World
```

To learn more about Ruby, visit http://www.ruby-lang.org.

PHP

PHP is a recursive acronym that stands for PHP: Hypertext Preprocessor, although when it was originally released PHP stood for Personal Home Page. Like Ruby, PHP was developed in

---

6 Posted on the ruby-talk mailing list in 1999.

the mid-1990s. Created by Rasmus Lerdorf to dynamically create web pages, it has become a popular scripting language for website designers.

PHP is an important part of the LAMP architecture. Seeing embedded PHP code within an HTML document is common. PHP can also be used as a standalone scripting language.

PHP Essentials

Is it installed?

```
root@centos:~# which php
/usr/bin/php
```

Install (if needed):

- Red Hat/Fedora/CentOS: `yum install php5`
- Debian/Mint/Ubuntu: `apt-get install php5`

Sample script— standalone example:

```
root@kali:~# more hello.php
#!/usr/bin/php
<?php
 echo "Hello, world\n";
?>
root@kali:~# chmod a+x hello.php
root@kali:~# ./hello.php
Hello World
```

Sample script— embedded HTML example:

```
<html>
 <head>
  <title>PHP Test</title>
 </head>
 <body>
 <?php echo '<p>Hello World</p>'; ?>
 </body>
</html>
```

To learn more about PHP, visit http://www.php.net.

JavaScript

In the mid-1990s the World Wide Web was just starting to become popular. An organization named Mosaic Communications (later becoming Netscape Communications) had just developed a graphical web browser and was exploring the possibility of using a programming language to enhance HTML. Initially they chose to incorporate Java. However, they soon decided that a scripting language would be a better solution.

JavaScript was designed to be similar to Java in terms of syntax. However, it is not a "spin-off" or extension of Java, but rather a scripting language that has similar syntax.

In addition to being heavily used, JavaScript is also used as an embedded scripting language in many products including Adobe Acrobat, MongoDB, and extensions for the Chrome and Opera web browsers.

JavaScript Essentials

Is it installed?

JavaScript is executed as part of the web browser, not typically installed. However, you can download and install an executable version from http://www. http://javascript-exe.com.

Sample script—embedded HTML example:

```
<html>
<head>
  <title></title>
</head>
<body>

<script>
console.log("hello world");
</script>
</body>
</html>
```

To learn more about JavaScript, visit https://developer.mozilla.org.

Tcl

Tcl[7] was created in the late 1980s by John Ousterhout. The tool was originally created for his students to use while he was a professor at the University of California, Berkeley. As additional features were added to the language and these students graduated, the popularity of the language grew.

In the early 1990s, the scripting language market was growing crowded and it was hard for a newer language to build traction. One of the main reasons Tcl became popular was the introduction of Tk, the Tool Kit extension to the Tcl language. Essentially a separate language itself, Tk made use of Tcl as a base language and added features that enabled developers to quickly

---

7   Originally Tool Command Language, Tcl is commonly referred to as tickle.

and easily create graphical-based, platform-independent programs. The combination of Tcl and Tk is referred to as Tcl/Tk.

Tcl/Tk Essentials

Is it installed (Tcl=tclsh, Tk=wish)?

```
root@centos:~# which tclsh
/usr/bin/tclsh
root@centos:~# which wish
/usr/bin/wish
```

Install (if needed):

- Red Hat/Fedora/CentOS: `yum install tcl`
- Red Hat/Fedora/CentOS: `yum install tk`
- Debian/Mint/Ubuntu: `apt-get install tcl`
- Debian/Mint/Ubuntu: `apt-get install tk`

Sample Tcl script:

```
root@centos:~# more hello.tcl
#!/usr/bin/tclsh
puts "Hello World"
root@centos:~# chmod a+x hello.tcl
root@centos:~# ./hello.tcl
Hello World
```

Sample Tk script:

```
root@centos:~# more hello.tk
#!/usr/bin/wish
button .hello -text "Hello World" -command { exit }
pack .hello
root@kali:~# chmod a+x hello.tk
root@kali:~# ./hello.tk
#Note: output is a graphical program
```

To learn more about Ruby, visit http://www.tcl.tk.

sed and awk

The `sed` and `awk` executables are command-line utilities that also have programming features. Typically, you use the `sed` command to parse a data stream (like a file) one line at a time and preform some sort of change to a document. For example, the following sed command replaces all numbers with an X character:[8]

```
root@centos:~# more /etc/hosts
127.0.0.1      localhost
127.0.1.1      centos

# The following lines are desirable for IPv6 capable hosts
::1     localhost ip6-localhost ip6-loopback
ff02::1 ip6-allnodes
ff02::2 ip6-allrouters

root@centos:~# sed 's/[0-9]/X/g' /etc/hosts
XXX.X.X.X      localhost
XXX.X.X.X      centos

# The following lines are desirable for IPvX capable hosts
::X     localhost ipX-localhost ipX-loopback
ffXX::X ipX-allnodes
ffXX::X ipX-allrouters
```

The awk utility is designed to work on database-based information, such as a system file. For example, consider the following data from the /etc/passwd file:

```
root@centos:~# head /etc/passwd
root:x:0:0:root:/root:/bin/bash
daemon:x:1:1:daemon:/usr/sbin:/usr/sbin/nologin
bin:x:2:2:bin:/bin:/usr/sbin/nologin
sys:x:3:3:sys:/dev:/usr/sbin/nologin
sync:x:4:65534:sync:/bin:/bin/sync
games:x:5:60:games:/usr/games:/usr/sbin/nologin
man:x:6:12:man:/var/cache/man:/usr/sbin/nologin
lp:x:7:7:lp:/var/spool/lpd:/usr/sbin/nologin
mail:x:8:8:mail:/var/mail:/usr/sbin/nologin
news:x:9:9:news:/var/spool/news:/usr/sbin/nologin
```

With the awk utility, we either display or modify fields of data. For example, to print just the user name (first field) and login shell (seventh field), use the following awk command:

```
root@centos:~# head /etc/passwd | awk -F : '{print $1, $7}'
root /bin/bash
daemon /usr/sbin/nologin
bin /usr/sbin/nologin
sys /usr/sbin/nologin
sync /bin/sync
games /usr/sbin/nologin
man /usr/sbin/nologin
```

---

8 Does the syntax 's/[0-9]/X/g' look familiar? It should remind you of the search and replace feature of the vi editor (see Chapter 5, "Text Editors"). This is because, like vi, sed was derived from older UNIX editors.

```
lp /usr/sbin/nologin
mail /usr/sbin/nologin
news /usr/sbin/nologin
```

Both sed and awk are not only powerful command-line utilities, but they also have simple programming features, such as variable usage and flow control. For more details on creating sed scripts, view the man page for sed or see https://www.gnu.org/software/sed/manual/sed.html. The awk utility also has a good man page in addition to the following website: https://www.gnu.org/software/gawk/manual/gawk.html.

Compiled Languages

The primary focus of this book is to introduce developers to Linux and languages that are specifically popular in Linux. Complied languages, such as C, C++, and Java[9] are not covered in great detail in this book for several reasons:

- These languages are huge topics and more difficult to learn than scripting languages.

- Although these languages certainly exist and are popular in Linux, they are even more widely used on non-Linux platforms, such as Microsoft Windows (particularly C++ and Microsoft's C#). In other words, they aren't languages that are primarily popular in Linux but standard languages commonly found on many platforms.

- The assumption is that you are already a developer and likely already know one or more of these complied languages.

Although this book won't include specifics on how to create C, C++, or Java programs, Chapter 11, "C, C++, and Java," does cover topics specifically related to writing code in these languages on Linux platforms. This includes the following:

- Handling system libraries
- Building packages
- Java installation

C Programming Basics

In the event that you are not familiar with the C language, here are some basics that you should be aware of:

- It's an older and well-established language.
- It lacks object-oriented features.

---

9 Technically Java isn't a complied language, but it belongs more in this category than the scripting language category.

- It is often used for low-level tasks, such as the Linux kernel.

- It typically requires much more coding because simple tasks require loading libraries.

- Code must be compiled for a specific operating system: Write Once, Compile Anywhere (WOCA).

C++ Programming Basics

In the event that you are not familiar with the C++ language, here are some basics that you should be aware of:

- It adds features to C.

- Its additional features include object-oriented programming.

- It's typically used for more complicated, high-level programming tasks.

- Code must be compiled for a specific operating system: Write Once, Compile Anywhere (WOCA).

Java Programming Basics

In the event that you are not familiar with the Java language, here are some basics that you should be aware of; it is

- An object-oriented language

- Designed to be more flexible than C++

- Runs via a "virtual machine," with the result being more portable code: Write Once, Run Anywhere/Everywhere (WORA/WORE)

IDEs

As a developer you might already be familiar with Integrated Development Environments (IDEs). For example, if you have developed C or C++ code on Microsoft Windows platforms, you are likely familiar with Microsoft Visual Studio.

An IDE provides you with tools to make the process of developing code easier. These tools could include a debugger program, a special editor that provides syntax highlighting and other features or features that enable you to insert new code quickly (and without error).

Many IDEs are available for Linux. Some are very specific to a language, whereas others are a bit more generic. It is also important to note that some of these IDEs are free, but others might require a fee of some sort to use them.

The goal of mentioning IDEs is to encourage you to explore what is available. Suppose, for example, you explore the different Linux programming languages and decide that Python is the best language for you. Before diving into the language further, explore the available IDEs (more than a dozen exist just for Python) and make a point to learn how to use the one that best meets your needs.[10]

> ### Programming Humor
>
> **Algorithm** (noun): Word used by software developers when they do not want to explain what their code does.

Summary

This chapter provided you with a foundation in programming languages that are commonly used on Linux distributions. You learned the difference between a scripting language and a structured language. You were also introduced to several different scripting languages that are popular on Linux. The topics described in this chapter lay the groundwork for the next four chapters in which you will learn more about BASH, Perl, and Python scripting as well as essentials regarding writing C, C++, and Java code on Linux distributions.

---

10 If you follow my advice on IDEs, you will not be sorry. I can't tell you how many developers I have spoken to who are using simple text editors to create their code and not taking advantage of great debugging tools that are available. They waste hours of time by using inadequate tools. Save yourself future headaches and find a good IDE now, not sometime in the future!

BASH Shell Scripting

The primary benefit of BASH scripting is that you can use everything that is available in the BASH shell within a BASH script. Because your Linux distribution has hundreds (maybe even thousands) of commands, each of which can be used in a BASH script, BASH shell scripting can be a very powerful tool.

This chapter focuses on providing you a firm understanding of how to write basic BASH scripts as well as introducing you to some of the more advanced features.

Basics of BASH Scripting

To an extent, you already know many of the basics of BASH scripting because you have already learned many features of the BASH shell in this book. For example, you learned about shell variables in Chapter 4, "Essential Commands." Shell variables are used in BASH scripting to store values.

To start a BASH script, enter the following as the first line of the script file:

```
#!/bin/bash
```

This special sequence is called the sha-bang, and it tells the system to execute this code as a BASH script.

The Story Behind sha-bang

To understand the origin of the term *sha-bang*, you first need to know two other slang terms. In Linux, a # character is called a hash and a ! character is called a bang. Put them together and you get hash-bang or sha-bang for short.

Some documentation referred to this as a *she-bang*, but because of the origin of the term, I think sha-bang makes more sense. In any case, you now know why #! is called sha-bang!

Comments in a BASH script start with a # character and extend to the end of the line. For example:

```
echo "hello world"   #prints "hello" to the screen
```

As shown in the preceding example, you can use the `echo` command to display information to the user who is running a program. The arguments to the echo command can contain any text data and can also include the value of a variable:

```
echo "The answer is $result"
```

After creating your BASH script and saving it, you then make it executable:

```
[student@OCS ~]$ more hello.sh
#!/bin/bash
#hello.sh


echo "hello world!"
[student@OCS ~]$ chmod a+x hello.sh
```

Now it can be run as a program by using the following syntax:

```
[student@OCS ~]$ ./hello.sh
hello world!
```

Note the need to place ./ before the name of the command. This is because the command might not be in one of the directories specified by the `$PATH` variable:

```
[student@OCS ~]$ echo $PATH
/usr/local/sbin:/usr/local/bin:/usr/sbin:/usr/bin:/sbin:/bin:/usr/games:/usr/local/
games
```

To avoid the need to include ./ whenever you want to run your script, you can modify the `$PATH` variable to include the directory in which your script is stored. Typically, regular users create a "bin" directory in their home directory and place scripts in this location:

```
[student@OCS ~]$ mkdir bin
[student@OCS ~]$ cp hello.sh bin
[student@OCS ~]$ PATH="$PATH:/home/student/bin"
[student@OCS ~]$ hello.sh
hello world!
```

In addition to the built-in variables that were discussed in Chapter 4, variables are available in BASH scripts that represent the arguments being passed into the script. For example, consider the following execution of a script called `test.sh`:

```
[student@OCS ~]$ test.sh Bob Sue Ted
```

The values "Bob," "Sue," and "Ted" are assigned to variables within the script. The first argument ("Bob") is assigned to the `$1` variable, the second argument is assigned to the `$2` variable, and so on. Additionally, all arguments collectively are assigned to the `$@` variable.

For additional details regarding these positional parameters variables, or anything related the BASH scripting, consult the man page for bash:

```
[student@OCS ~]$ man bash
```

Conditional Expressions

Several conditional statements are available for the BASH shell, including the `if` statement:

```
if [ cond ]
then
    statements
elif [ cond ]
then
    statement
else
    statements
fi
```

Note the following:

- An else if is spelled `elif` and is optional.

- After the `if` and `elif`, you need a `then` statement. However, after an `else`, do not include a **then** statement.

- End the `if` statement with the word *if* spelled backwards: `fi`

See Listing 8.1 for an example of an `if` statement.

Listing 8.1   **Sample `if` statement**

```
#!/bin/bash
#if.sh

color=$1

if [ "$color" = "blue" ]
then
    echo "it is blue"
elif [ "$color" = "red" ]
then
    echo "it is red"
else
    echo "no idea what this color is"
fi
```

Listing 8.1 used the following conditional statement:

```
[ "$color" = "blue" ]
```

Quoting variables

Get in the habit of putting double quotes around your variables in BASH scripts. This is important in the event the variable hasn't been assigned a value. For example, suppose the script in Listing 8.1 was execute with no arguments. The result would be that the color variable is unassigned and the resulting conditional statement would be `if [ "" = "blue" ]`

The result would be false, but without the quotes around `$color`, the result would be an error message and the script would exit immediately. This is because the resulting conditional statement would be missing one of its key components after the value of `$color` has been returned: `if [ = "blue" ]`

This syntax performs an implicit call of a BASH command named `test` that you can use to perform several comparison tests. This can include integer (numeric) comparisons, string comparisons, and file testing operations.[1] For example, use the following syntax to test whether the string value that is stored in the `$name1` variable does not equal the string stored in the `$name2` variable:

```
[ "$name1" != "$name2" ]
```

Important Note

The spacing around the square brackets is very important. There should be a space before and after each square bracket. Without these, an error message occurs.

In addition to determining whether two strings are equal or not equal to each other, you might also find the `-n` option useful.[2] This option determines whether a string is not empty, which is useful when testing user input. For example, the code in Listing 8.2 reads data from user input (the keyboard), assigns the input to the `$name` variable, and tests to make sure the user typed something for the name.

Listing 8.2 **Testing user input**

```
[student@OCS ~]$ more name.sh
#!/bin/bash
#name.sh

echo "Enter your name"
read name

if [ -n "$name" ]
then
    echo "Thank you!"
else
    echo "hey, you didn't give a name!"
fi
[student@OCS ~]$./name.sh
Enter your name
```

---

1 See the man page for `test` to learn more about its comparison operations: **man test**

2 A similar option, `-z`, returns true if the string contains zero characters.

```
Bo
Thank you!
[student@OCS ~]$./name.sh
Enter your name
hey, you didn't give a name!
```

Integer Comparisons

If you want to perform integer (numeric) comparison operations, use the following:

- `-eq` True if values are equal to each other.

- `-ne` True if values are not equal to each other.

- `-gt` True if first value is greater than second value.

- `-lt` True if first value is less than second value.

- `-ge` True if first value is greater than or equal to second value.

- `-le` True if first value is less than or equal to second value.

File Test Comparisons

You can also perform test operations on files and directories to determine information about their status. These operations include:

- `-d` True if "file" is a directory.

- `-f` True if "file" is a regular file.

- `-r` True if "file" exists and is readable by the user running the script.

- `-w` True if "file" exists and is writable by the user running the script.

- `-x` True if "file" exists and is executable by the user running the script.

- `-L` True if "first" value is less than or equal to second value.

Flow Control Statements

In addition to `if` statements, the BASH scripting language has several other flow control statements:

- **The `while` loop**—Executes a block of code repeatedly as long as the conditional statement is true.

- **The `until` loop**—Executes a block of code repeatedly as long as the conditional statement is false. Essentially the opposite of a `while` loop.

- **The `case` statement**—Similar to an `if` statement but provides an easier branching method for multiple situations.

- **The `for` loop**—Executes a block of code for each item of a list of values.

The `while` loop

The following code segment prompts the user for a five-digit number. If the user complies, the program will continue because the condition of the while loop will be false. However, if the user provides incorrect data, the condition of the `while` loop will be true and the user will be prompted for the correct data again:

```
echo "Enter a five-digit ZIP code: "
read ZIP

while echo $ZIP | egrep -v "^[0-9]{5}$" > /dev/null 2>&1
do
    echo "You must enter a valid ZIP code - five digits only!"
    echo "Enter a five-digit ZIP code: "
    read ZIP
done

echo "Thank you"
```

The `egrep` command from the previous example may be a bit tricky to understand. To begin with, the regular expression pattern is matching a value that is exactly five digits. The –v option is used to return a value if the pattern is not found. So, if `$ZIP` contains a valid five-digit number, then `egrep` returns a false result because it is trying to find lines that don't contain a five-digit number. The `egrep` command returns a true result if the `$ZIP` contains something besides a five-digit number.

Why the `> /dev/null 2>&1`? Because we don't want to display anything from the `egrep` command, just make use of its true/false return value. All OS commands return true or false[3] when executed, and that is what is needed here. Any STDOUT or STDERR from the command is unnecessary and only serves to confuse matters if it is displayed to the user.

The `for` Loop

A `for` loop enables you to perform an operation on a set of items. For example, the following command, when run as the root user, creates five user accounts:

```
for person in bob ted sue nick fred
do
    useradd $person
done
```

> **Loop Control**
>
> Like most languages, BASH scripting provides a way to prematurely exit a loop or to stop the current iteration of a loop and start a new iteration of a loop. Use the `break` command to immediately exit a `while`, `until`, or `for` loop. Use the `continue` command to stop the current iteration of a `while`, `until`, or `for` loop and start the next iteration.

---

3 Technically they return 0 for "true" and a positive number for "false."

The `case` Statement

A `case` statement is designed for when you want to perform multiple conditional checks. Although you could use an `if` statement with multiple `elif` statements, the syntax of `if/elif/else` is often more cumbersome than a `case` statement.

The syntax for a case statement is:

```
case var in
cond1)  cmd
            cmd;;
cond2)  cmd
            cmd;;
esac
```

For the preceding syntax example, `var` represents a variable's value that you want to conditionally check. For example, consider the following code:

```
name="bob"

case $name in
ted)  echo "it is ted";;
bob) echo "it is bob";;
*)      echo "I have no idea who you are"
esac
```

The "condition" is a pattern that uses the same matching rules as file wildcards. An `*` matches zero or more of any character, a `?` matches a single character, and you can use square brackets to match a single character of a specific range. You can also use a `|` character to represent "or." For example, consider Listing 8.3, which is used to check a user's answer to a question:

Listing 8.3   **Example of the `case` statement**

```
answer=yes

case $answer in
y|ye[sp]) echo "you said yes";;
n|no|nope) echo "you said no";;
*)  echo "bad response";;
esac
```

User Interaction

The example in Listing 8.3 is a bit of a puzzle because it is intended to check user input. However, the variable is hard coded. Using actual user input, which the `read` statement can gather, would make more sense:

```
read answer
```

The `read` statement prompts the user to provide information and reads that data (technically from STDIN) into a variable that is specified as the argument to the `read` statement. See Listing 8.4 for an example.

Listing 8.4   **Example of the `read` statement**

```
read answer

case $answer in
y|ye[sp]) echo "you said yes";;
n|no|nope) echo "you said no";;
*)  echo "bad response";;
esac
```

Additional Information

Do you want to learn more about creating BASH scripts? The following are good resources for additional information:

- **man bash**—The man page for the BASH shell has a great deal of information about writing BASH scripts.

- **http://tldp.org**—A website that is (sadly) mostly out of date.[4] However, it has one gem of a document called the "Advanced Bash-Scripting Guide." Click on the Guides link under the Documents section and scroll down until you see this guide. The author of this guide normally updates it on a regular basis. Because the guides are listed by publication date, this guide is almost always at the top of the list.

> **BASH Scripting Humor**
>
> This isn't technically a script humor item, but because you will likely be editing files using the vim editor...
>
> Open the vim editor by executing the command vim at the command line. Then type `:help 42`.

Summary

This book does not cover some additional features of BASH scripting. However, the goal of this chapter was to provide you with enough information to determine whether BASH scripting is a good language for you. If you liked the features and syntax of BASH scripting, consider exploring the documentation provided to learn more about this flexible language.

---

4 It has a few up-to-date documents, but most are very much outdated. Look at the publication date of the document and realize that anything older than a couple of years is probably no longer accurate (but still might provide you with some useful information).

Perl Scripting

Although Perl might have started as a simple scripting language, it has grown into a robust language designed to tackle many different coding situations. There is a great deal to learn about Perl scripting (as well as the other programming languages discussed in this book), so don't expect to become an expert overnight.

This chapter's focus is to give you a firm understanding of how to write basic Perl scripts as well as provide an understanding of some of Perl's more advanced features.

Basics of Perl Scripting

Perl is an unstructured language, which means white space within the program is typically ignored. For example, the following code prints "hi" to the screen:

```
print "hi\n";
```

This could also be written as follows:[1]

```
print
"hi\n"

          ;
```

Note that a semicolon (;) is used to end a statement in Perl. Also note that the \n string represents a newline character. The print statement doesn't naturally display a newline character, which makes for awkward output when multiple print statements are executed.

Comments in Perl begin with a pound sign character (#) and extend to the end of the line. For example:

```
# This is my first Perl script
print "hello\n";   #displays "hello"
```

---

1   Just because it could be written this way doesn't mean you should write your code like this. As with all languages, you should try to write Perl code that is easy to read.

Executing Perl Code

In most cases, you place Perl code within a file and execute the code as shown in the following:

```
[student@OCS ~]$ more hello.pl
print "hello\n";
[student@OCS ~]$ perl hello.pl
hello
```

Typing the `perl` command before each execution can become annoying. To avoid that, make use of the `#!` line:

```
[student@OCS ~]$ more hello.pl
#!/bin/perl

print "hello\n";
[student@OCS ~]$ chmod a+x hello.pl
[student@OCS ~]$ ./hello.pl
hello
```

You can also make use of a feature called the Perl debugger to execute Perl code interactively. Start by executing the following command: `perl -d -e "1;"`

The `-d` option enters the Perl debugger, which requires valid Perl code. The `-e` option means "execute the code provided on the command line." The `"1;"` is valid Perl code; it doesn't do anything but return the value of true. The result of this command should be a prompt like the one shown in Listing 9.1.

Listing 9.1 **The interactive Perl debugger**

```
[student@OCS ~]$ perl -d -e "1;"

Loading DB routines from perl5db.pl version 1.37
Editor support available.

Enter h or 'h h' for help, or 'man perldebug' for more help.

main::(-e:1):   1;
    DB<1>
```

At the `DB<1` prompt you can type a Perl statement. Press the Enter key to execute the command. This enables you to test Perl code interactively.[2] A couple of things to note:

- Normally you need to place a `;` character after each Perl statement. In the Perl debugger, the Enter key acts like a `;` character. This means you don't need a `;` character at the end of a Perl statement within the debugger.

---

2 This method also provides a way for me to demonstrate Perl features without having to create a full Perl script.

- A few things don't work in the Perl debugger (for example, a regular expression feature called **backreferencing**). However, almost everything that works in a Perl script also works in the interactive Perl debugger.

- To exit the Perl debugger, type **q** and then press the ENTER key.

Additional Perl Documentation

Perl is a language that offers a large number of features, well beyond what is covered in this book (or any book for that matter). Fortunately, you can use a number of resources to get additional information about Perl:

- **perldoc.perl.org**—Primary documentation website.

- **man perl**—On UNIX and Linux systems, this command provides details about Perl.

- **perldoc**—On all platforms, this command provides information about Perl.

The `perldoc` command is especially useful. Try running the following command:
`perldoc perl`

Man page-like output appears that provides information about Perl. Included in this is a list of additional categories as shown in Figure 9.1.

```
Overview
      perl                Perl overview (this section)
      perlintro           Perl introduction for beginners
      perltoc             Perl documentation table of contents

Tutorials
      perlreftut          Perl references short introduction
      perldsc             Perl data structures intro
      perllol             Perl data structures: arrays of arrays

      perlrequick         Perl regular expressions quick start
      perlretut           Perl regular expressions tutorial

      perlootut           Perl OO tutorial for beginners

      perlperf            Perl Performance and Optimization Techniques

      perlstyle           Perl style guide

      perlcheat           Perl cheat sheet
      perltrap            Perl traps for the unwary
      perldebtut          Perl debugging tutorial

      perlfaq             Perl frequently asked questions
        perlfaq1          General Questions About Perl
        perlfaq2          Obtaining and Learning about Perl
        perlfaq3          Programming Tools
```

Figure 9.1   Perl help topics

So, if you want to learn about Perl regular expressions, you could execute the `perldoc`
`perlrequick` or `perldoc perlretut` commands. You can view dozens of different categories
to learn more about Perl. As you learn more details about Perl while reading this book, consider
diving into this documentation as well.

Variables and Values

Perl has three data structure types:

- **Scalar**—A single data type that can be used as either a string or a number.

- **Array**—An ordered list of scalar values, separated by commas.

- **Hash**—A collection of unordered values that are referenced by using a scalar key. Also
  called an associate array.

Scalar variables are assigned and referenced using a $ character:

```
[student@localhost Desktop]$ perl -d -e "1;"

Loading DB routines from perl5db.pl version 1.37
Editor support available.

Enter h or 'h h' for help, or 'man perldebug' for more help.

main::(-e:1):  1;
  DB<1> $name="Bob"
  DB<2> print $name
Bob
```

> **Note**
>
> To read data from the user (the keyboard), use the syntax $name=<STDIN>;

Several useful built-in Perl statements are used on scalars, including the statements shown
in Listing 9.2.

Listing 9.2 **Useful scalar statements**

```
[student@localhost Desktop]$ perl -d -e "1;"

Loading DB routines from perl5db.pl version 1.37
Editor support available.

Enter h or 'h h' for help, or 'man perldebug' for more help.
```

.

```
main::(-e:1):  1;
  DB<1> $name=<STDIN>       #grabs data from keyboard and assigns to $name
Bob Smith
  DB<2> print $name         #prints "Bob Smith\n"; \n is a newline character
Bob Smith
  DB<3> chomp $name         #removes newline character at the end of string
  DB<4> print $name         #prints "Bob Smith" without newline character
Bob Smith
  DB<5> $name=lc ($name)  #returns lower case "bob smith"
  DB<6> print $name
bob smith
```

Arrays are defined by creating variables that begin with an @ character:

```
  DB<1> @colors=("red", "blue", "green")
  DB<2> print "@colors"
red blue green
```

One confusing element of Perl is how you refer to individual elements in an array. Because those individual elements are scalar values, you use a $ character to display a single value. For example, to display the first element in an array you do something like the following:

```
  DB<1> @colors=("red", "blue", "green")
  DB<2> print $colors[0]
red
```

Important statements that manipulate arrays include the following:

- push—Adds a new element to end of the array

- unshift—Adds a new element to beginning of the array

- pop—Removes (and returns) the last element of the array

- shift—Removes (and returns) the first element of the array

- splice—Add or remove one or more items in any part of the array

- sort—Sorts elements in an array

You can perform an operation on each element in an array by using the foreach statement:

```
  DB<1> @names=("Smith", "Jones", "Rothwell")
  DB<2> foreach $person (@names) {print "Hello, Mr. $person\n";}
Hello, Mr. Smith
Hello, Mr. Jones
Hello, Mr. Rothwell
```

Creating an array can be a pain because of all the quotes[3] and commas. To make life easier, use the qw or qq statements:

```
DB<1> @colors=qq(red blue green) #same as @colors=("red", "blue", "green")
DB<2> @colors=qw(red blue green) #same as @colors=('red', 'blue', 'green')
```

Single versus Double Quotes

A double-quoted string allows for special characters whereas a single-quoted string does not. For example, the string `"hello\n"` means `hello` followed by a newline character (`\n` = newline character). However, the string `'hello\n'` means `hello\n`.

A **hash** (called a **dictionary** in some other languages) provides a way to associate a key with a value. For example, to keep track of the favorite color of some people, you could use the following code:

```
DB<1> %favorite=("Sue" => "blue", "Ted" => "green", "Nick" => "black")
DB<2> print $favorite{"Ted"}
green
```

To see all the keys in a hash, use the keys command:

```
DB<1> %favorite=("Sue" => "blue", "Ted" => "green", "Nick" => "black")
DB<2> @people=keys(%favorite)
DB<3> print "@people"
Ted Nick Sue
```

Special Variables

Several variables in Perl have a special meaning to the language. Typically these variables have cryptic names, such as `$|` or `$_`. For example, the `$$` variable contains the process ID of the Perl process itself.

Some of these variables hold important information whereas others can be modified to change the behavior of how Perl functions. To see a description of all of these special variables, visit this URL: http://perldoc.perl.org/perlvar.html.

Flow Control

Perl supports many traditional flow control statements, including the if statement:[4]

```
$name=<STDIN>;
chomp $name;
```

---

3 Yes, you should use quotes around strings, even though it seems like you don't need them in Perl. By default, Perl tries to use an unquoted value as a function and replaces the function call with the return value of the function. Placing quotes around the string prevents function calls.

4 Note the formatting of this code. Perl really doesn't care about formatting, but someone reading your code will. There is no standard convention as to how you format your Perl code, but I suggest that you at least be consistent within the program that you are writing to make it easier to read.

```
if ($name eq "Tim")
    {
        print "Welcome, Tim!";
    }
elsif ($name eq "Bob")
    {
        print "Welcome, Bob!";
    }
else
    {
        print "Welcome, stranger!";
    }
```

elsif?

Be careful when writing Perl `if` statements because the "else if" statement is oddly spelled. It is a single word, with the second "e" missing!

Another common conditional statement is the `while` loop. With the `while` loop, a conditional check is performed and, if the condition is true, a block of code is executed. After the block of code is executed, the conditional check is performed again. See Listing 9.3 for an example.

Listing 9.3 **The `while` loop**

```
print "Enter your age: ";
$age=<STDIN>;
chomp $age;

#Make sure the user entered a proper age:
while ($age < 0)
{
   print "You can't be that young!\n";
   print "Enter your age: ";
   $age=<STDIN>;
   chomp $age;
}
print "Thank you!\n";
```

Additional flow control statements include the following:

- `until`—Opposite of the `while` statement; executes a block of code as long as the conditional statement returns false.

- `unless`—Opposite of the `if` statement; executes a block of code if the conditional statement is false.

- `for`—Designed to perform a specific number of operations. Example:

    `for ($i=1; $i <=10; $i++) {#code}`
- `foreach`—Performs a block of code for each item of a list (array).

> ### What about Switch or Case Statements?
>
> Natively, Perl doesn't have a switch or case statement. You might see older Perl code make use of multiple `if/elsif` statements or clever use of other conditional statements to simulate a `switch` statement. However, modern Perl provides a means to access a switch-like statement called `given`:
>
> ```
> use feature "switch";
>
>     given ($setting) {
>         when (/^Code/) { $code = 1 }
>         when (/^Test/) { $test = 1 }
>         default       { $neither = 1 }
>     }
> ```
>
> The `^Code` and `^Test` are regular expressions and are covered later in this chapter.

Many languages support loop control statements such as `break` and `continue`. Perl also supports loop control statements, but they are called `last` and `next` instead of `break` and `continue`. You can use these loop controls statements in `while`, `until for`, and `foreach` loops.

Conditions

Perl supports a large variety of conditional expressions, including numeric comparison, string comparison, file testing operations, and regular expressions. You can also use the outcome of a Perl statement, but be aware that only a handful of built-in Perl statements return a natural true or false value.

Numeric comparisons include the following:

- `==` Determine whether two numbers are equal to each other.

  Example:
  ```
  if ($age == 35) {}
  ```

- `!=` Determine whether two numbers are not equal to each other.

  Example:
  ```
  if ($age != 35) {}
  ```

- `<` Determine whether one number is less than another number.

  Example:
  ```
  if ($age < 35) {}
  ```

- `<=` Determine whether one number is less than or equal to another number.

  Example:
  ```
  if ($age <= 35) {}
  ```

- `>` Determine whether one number is greater than another number.

  Example:
  ```
  if ($age > 35) {}
  ```

- `>=` Determine whether one number is greater than or equal to another number.

  Example:
  ```
  if ($age >= 35) {}
  ```

String comparisons include:

- `eq` Determine whether two scalars are equal to each other.

  Example:
  ```
  if ($name eq "Bob") {}
  ```

- `ne` Determine whether two scalars are not equal to each other.

  Example:
  ```
  if ($name ne "Bob") {}
  ```

- `lt` Determine whether one scalar is less than another scalar.

  Example:
  ```
  if ($name lt "Bob") {}
  ```

- `le` Determine whether one scalar is less than or equal to another scalar.

  Example:
  ```
  if ($name le "Bob") {}
  ```

- `gt` Determine whether one scalar is greater than another scalar.

  Example:
  ```
  if ($name gt "Bob") {}
  ```

- `ge` Determine whether one scalar is greater than or equal to another scalar.

  Example:
  ```
  if ($name ge "Bob") {}
  ```

File test operators include:[5]

- `-r` Determine whether a file is readable. Example: if (-r "file") {}

- `-w` Determine whether a file is writable

---

5 Note that when you look at Perl documentation, file test operators are not listed in the section regarding operators, but rather under the "Functions" section. Look for –X under functions to learn more about file test operators.

- `-x`   Determine whether a file is executable

- `-T`   Determine whether a file contains text data

- `-e`   Determine whether a file exists

- `-f`   Determine whether a file exists and is a plain file

- `-d`   Determine whether a file exists and is a directory[6]

Regular expressions are a powerful feature in the Perl programming language. For example, you can see whether a pattern exists inside of a scalar variable by using the following code:

```
$name=<STDIN>;
if ($name =~ m/Bob/)
{
    print "yes"
}
```

When reading Perl code, you should be aware of a few regular expression features:

- You can also perform substitution by using the following syntax:

  ```
  $name =~ s/Bob/Ted
  ```

- This replaced "Bob" with "Ted" in the $name variable.

- Because matching is more common than substitution, you can drop the "m" when performing a match:

  ```
  if ($name =~ /Bob/) {}
  ```

- The $_ variable is called the default variable and is often used by default. For example:

  ```
  if ($_ =~ /Bob/) {} is the same as if (/Bob/) {}
  ```

Additional Features

In addition to reading from the keyboard (STDIN), you can open files and read directly from the files. This is referred to as opening a filehandle:[7]

```
open (DATA, "<file.txt");
$line=<DATA>;
close DATA;     #when finished, close the filehandle
```

You can also open a file and write to the file:

```
open (DATA, ">file.txt");
print DATA "This is output";
```

---

6 I know the wording of this seems odd, but a directory is technically a file in Linux. It is a file that contains specific data, a list of files that are in the directory.

7 Several techniques actually exist for reading from a file. This is just one of them.

```
close DATA;    #when finished, close the filehandle
```

Another important feature in Perl is functions. To create a function, use the following syntax:

```
sub welcome
{
   print "This is my function";
}
```

You can call a function by using the following syntax:

```
&welcome;
```

By default, any variable created in the main part of the program is available in a function. Additionally, any variable in a function is available in the main part of the program:

```
sub total
{
    $z=$x + $y;    #  $x and $y from main program
}

$x=10;
$y=5;
&total;
print $z;    #  $z from total subroutine
```

To make variables private, use the my statement:[8]

```
sub total
{
    my $z=$x + $y;    #  $x and $y are not set here
}

my $x=10;
my $y=5;
&total;
print $z;    #  $z is not set here
```

To reuse code in other programs, Perl has a feature called **modules**. Modules are like libraries in other languages. By calling a module, you will have access to functions that are shared by that module to your program.

For example, the following module call provides a function called cwd, which displays the current directory:

```
[student@OCS ~]$ perl -d -e "1;"

Loading DB routines from perl5db.pl version 1.37
Editor support available.
```

---

8 This is a very simplistic view of variable scope in Perl. In reality, Perl provides you with the capability to have a much more robust (and complex) scoping process.

```
Enter h or 'h h' for help, or 'man perldebug' for more help.

main::(-e:1):  1;
  DB<1> use Cwd;
  DB<2> print cwd;
/home/student
```

A few things to note about modules:

- By convention, module names begin with a capital letter. If you see a `use` statement that calls something that is in all lowercase characters, it isn't a module, but rather another Perl feature called a **pragma**. Pragmas are used to change the default behavior of Perl and are well documented on perldoc.perl.org in the "Pragmas" section.

- Perl comes with literally hundreds of built-in modules that enhance the functionality of the language greatly. These are all well documented on perldoc.perl.org in the "Modules" section.

- Which functions are provided by the module depend on the developer who created the module. View the module documentation to determine which functions are provided.

- You can create your own modules, but that topic is beyond the scope of this book. See perldoc.perl.org → language → perlmodlib for details.

Perl Humor

Larry Wall continues to oversee further development of Perl and serves as the benevolent dictator for life of the Perl project. His role in Perl is best conveyed by the so-called 2 Rules, taken from the official Perl documentation:

1. Larry is always by definition right about how Perl should behave. This means he has final veto power on the core functionality.

2. Larry is allowed to change his mind about any matter at a later date, regardless of whether he previously invoked Rule 1.

Got that? Larry is always right, even when he was wrong.

Summary

As a robust language, Perl has many additional features that were not covered in this chapter. However, the goal of this chapter was to provide you with enough information to determine whether Perl is a good language for you. If you liked the features and syntax of Perl, considering exploring the documentation sources provided to learn more about this flexible language.

10

Python Scripting

Python is a robust programming language that provides many different features that you would expect from a modern language. One of its many benefits is the fact that it is object-oriented by nature, making it a good language for large task programs.

This chapter's focus is to give you a firm understanding of how to write basic Python scripts as well as provide you with an understanding of some of Python's more advanced features.

Basics of Python Scripting

Unlike Perl (discussed in Chapter 9, "Perl Scripting"), Python is very much a structured language. It is very sensitive to white space, to the point that improper white space usage causes a program to crash with compile errors.

When you create a block of code, you must indent the entire block with the same number of white space characters. For example, consider the following code fragment, focusing on how the code is indented:

```
x = 25
if x > 15:
    print x
    a = 1
else:
print x
    a = 2
```

The preceding code fragment results in a compile time error message because the second print statement isn't properly indented. The positive thing about enforced structure is that it makes your code easier to read (for both others and yourself when you look over code that you wrote months or years ago). The negative thing is that it can be a pain when you miss a space or accidently use a tab instead of four spaces.[1]

---

1 You might be thinking, "Why did he say four spaces and not five or eight?" Python Enhancement Proposals (PEPs) are a major component of Python development. PEP8 is the "Style Guide for Python Code," and it states that the standard for indentation is four spaces.

> ### Use an Editor to Avoid Indentation Issues
>
> To avoid issues with indentation, use an editor designed to perform auto indentation. Many such editors are designed specifically for Python, but you can also use a generic editor such as vim.
>
> To enable auto indentation in vim, start the editor and then execute the command `:set autoindent`. Bonus: If you edit a file that ends with .py, the `vim` editor will color code key Python statements.

Executing Python Code

Currently, the two primary versions of Python are 2.x and 3.x. At the time of the writing of this book, version 2.x was the more popular of the two, so the book covers 2.x syntax. To determine which version of Python is installed on your Linux distribution, execute the `python` command with the `-v` option or enter the Python interactive shell by executing the `python` command with no arguments:

```
[student@OCS ~]$ python
Python 2.7.5 (default, Oct 11 2015, 17:47:16)
[GCC 4.8.3 20140911 (Red Hat 4.8.3-9)] on linux2
Type "help", "copyright", "credits" or "license" for more information.
>>> quit()
[student@OCS ~]$
```

Note that the `python` command not only displays the version of Python, but it also places you into an interactive Python shell where you can test Python code on the fly. To exit this Python shell, enter the `quit()` statement as shown in the previous example.

To execute a Python script that is stored in a file, use the following syntax:

```
[student@OCS ~]$ python script.py
```

Typing the `python` command before each execution can become annoying. To avoid that, make use of the `#!` line:

```
[student@OCS ~]$ more hello.py
#!/bin/python

print "hello"
[student@OCS ~]$ chmod a+x hello.py
[student@OCS ~]$ ./hello.py
hello
```

As demonstrated from the previous example, the `print` statement in Python is used to produce output. By default, this output goes to STDOUT.

> ### A Note about `.pyc` and `.pyo` Files
>
> Your Python script names should end with `.py`. You will sometimes also see files that end in `.pyc`, and this can lead to some confusion. Not touching these files is best because they are compiled versions of Python code and not something that you can edit directly.

These files are created when a Python library is called. The idea is that the compile process takes time and each time a library is called, its code would have to be compiled. To make the process more efficient, Python automatically saves this code into files that end in .pyc. So, if you call a library called input.py, you should expect to see a file called `input.pyc` after the program that calls the library is executed.

When Python is invoked with the -O option, a `.pyo` file is generated. Like `.pyc` files, this is compiled code, but it is optimized complied code.

Additional Documentation

Initially you probably want to look at the man page for python: `man python`. This provides you with some of the basics of the `python` executable, but there isn't much focus on how to write code in Python.

However, at the bottom of the python man page are some very useful links to additional documentation, as shown in Figure 10.1.

```
INTERNET RESOURCES
        Main website:  http://www.python.org/
        Documentation: http://docs.python.org/
        Developer resources:  http://docs.python.org/devguide/
        Downloads:  http://python.org/download/
        Module repository:  http://pypi.python.org/
        Newsgroups:  comp.lang.python, comp.lang.python.announce
```

Figure 10.1   Python documentation

The URL http://docs.python.org/ will likely be the most useful resource when you start learning Python, but the other links will also prove valuable over time.

Variables and Values

Python has several data structure types, including:

- **Numeric variables**—A single data type that is used to store numeric values.

- **String variables**—A single data type that is used to store string values.

- **Lists**—An ordered list of numeric or string values.

- **Dictionaries**—A collection of unordered values that are referenced by using a key.

Numbers and strings are different in that you can perform certain operations on numbers (addition, subtraction, and so on) but not on strings as demonstrated in Listing 10.1.

Listing 10.1 **Numbers versus strings**

```
[student@localhost Desktop]$ python
Python 2.7.5 (default, Oct 11 2015, 17:47:16)
[GCC 4.8.3 20140911 (Red Hat 4.8.3-9)] on linux2
Type "help", "copyright", "credits" or "license" for more information.
>>> a=100
>>> print a
100
>>> b=200
>>> print a + b
300
>>> c="hello"
>>> print a + c
Traceback (most recent call last):
  File "<stdin>", line 1, in <module>
TypeError: unsupported operand type(s) for +: 'int' and 'str'
```

Note the error that occurred in the last statement of Listing 10.1 when the string variable was used in a numeric operation.

Python has a rich set of operations that can be performed on strings. For example, you can use the following to capitalize a string:

```
>>> name="ted"
>>> name=name.capitalize()
>>> print name
Ted
```

Python is an object-oriented language. Variables store typed objects (numeric type, string type, and so on), and to call a method on an object, you use the notation *var*.*method*(). So, name. capitalize() calls the capitalize method on the object in the name variable.

Note that Python has a few traditional functions as well. For example, consider the following code:

```
>>> name="ted"
>>> print len(name)
3
```

The len function takes an object as an argument and returns the length of the object. Granted, using both method calls and functions can sometimes be confusing, but keep in mind that most of Python consists of method calls, and functions are fairly rare.

To create a list, use the following syntax:

```
>>> colors=["red", "blue", "yellow", "green"]
>>> print colors
['red', 'blue', 'yellow', 'green']
```

Use the following notation to access elements in a list:

```
>>> colors=["red", "blue", "yellow", "green"]
>>> print colors[1]
blue
>>> print colors[1:3]
['blue', 'yellow']
```

Important methods that manipulate lists include the following:

- `append`—Adds a new element to the end of the list.

- `insert`—Adds a new element to a specific position in the list.

- `extend`—Adds the elements of a list to another list.

- `del`—Removes an element from a list based on an index position.

- `pop`—Removes the last element from a list.

- `remove`—Removes an element from a list based the value of the element.

The Tuple

You are likely to come across another data structure that works much like a list called a **tuple**. Consider a tuple to be a list that, once created, can't be modified. Technically, tuples are **immutable**, a fancy way of saying unchangeable. They are a clever way of having constant-like data structures.

To create a dictionary in Python, use the following syntax:

```
>>> age={'Sarah': 25, "Julia": 18, "Nick": 107}
>>> print age
{'Sarah': 25, 'Nick': 107, 'Julia': 18}
>>> print age['Sarah']
25
```

To add a key-value pair to a dictionary, use the following syntax:

```
>>> age['Bob']=42
```

Times occur when you will want to get a list of all the keys of a dictionary. To accomplish this, use the `keys()` method:[2]

```
>>> age={'Sarah': 25, "Julia": 18, "Nick": 107}
>>> print age.keys()
['Sarah', 'Nick', 'Julia']
```

---

2 Note that the return value of the keys are not in the order they were originally created in. Remember that a dictionary is an unordered collection of key-value pairs.

> **Other Data Structures**
>
> Python has other data structures that you should consider exploring. For example, you can create sets of data within Python. This is useful because set objects have methods that enable you to find items that appear in two sets or items that only appear in a specific set.

Flow Control

Python supports many traditional flow control statements, including the `if` statement:

```
age=15
if age >= 16:
    print "you are old enough to drive"
elif age == 15:
    print "you are old enough for a permit"
else:
    print "sorry, you can't drive yet"
```

Another common conditional statement is the `while` loop. With the `while` loop, a conditional check is performed and, if the condition is true, a block of code is executed. After the block of code is executed, the conditional check is performed again. See Listing 10.2 for an example.

Listing 10.2 **The `while` loop**

```
#!/bin/python

age = int(raw_input('Please enter your age: '))

while (age < 0):
    print "You can't be that young!";
    age = int(raw_input('Please enter your age: '))

print "Thank you!";
```

Note that in Listing 10.2, the `raw_input()` function gets data from the user (STDIN, likely the keyboard) and the `int()` function converts this data into an integer object.

To perform an operation on each item of a list, use the `for` loop:

```
>>> colors=["red", "blue", "yellow", "green"]
>>> for hue in colors:
...     print hue
...
red
blue
yellow
green
```

Many languages support loop control statements such as `break` and `continue`. Python has these statements, which you can use in `while` loops or `for` loops. The `break` statement exits the loop prematurely and the `continue` statement stops the current iteration of the loop and starts the next iteration. Python also supports an `else` statement that you can use to execute additional code if the loop is terminated without a `break` statement.

Conditions

Python supports a large variety of conditional expressions, which enable you to perform comparison operations on like objects. For example, you can compare strings to strings, dictionaries to dictionaries, and so on.

Comparison operators include the following:

- `==` Determine whether two objects are equal to each other.

- `!=` Determine whether two objects are not equal to each other.

- `<` Determine whether one object is less than another object.

- `<=` Determine whether one object is less than or equal to another object.

- `>` Determine whether one object is greater than another object.

- `>=` Determine whether one object is greater than or equal to another object.

Additional Features

In addition to reading from the keyboard, you can open files and read directly from the files. For example:

```
>>> data=open('test.py', 'r')
>>> print data
<open file 'test.py', mode 'r' at 0x7f4db20ba1e0>
```

The first argument to the `open` statement is the filename to open. The second argument is how to open it. The value `'r'` means to open the file for reading. You can also open a file and write to the file by using the value of `'w'`.

You can use several methods for reading from and writing to a file after opening it:

- `read()`—Reads the entire file. Example: `total = data.read()`.

- `readline`—Reads one line from the file.

- `write`—Writes data to a file. Example: `data.write("hello")`.

Another important feature in Python is functions. To create a function, use the following syntax:

```
def welcome():
   print "This is my function"
```

You can call a function by using the following syntax:

```
welcome()
```

To reuse code in other programs, Perl has a feature called **modules**. By calling a module, you have access to functions that are shared by that module in your program.

For example, the following module call provides a function called `path` that displays a list of directories where Python libraries are held:

```
>>> import sys
>>> print sys.path
['', '/usr/lib64/python27.zip', '/usr/lib64/python2.7', '/usr/lib64/python2.7/plat-
linux2', '/usr/lib64/python2.7/lib-tk', '/usr/lib64/python2.7/lib-old', '/usr/lib64/
python2.7/lib-dynload', '/usr/lib64/python2.7/site-packages', '/usr/lib64/python2.7/
site-packages/gtk-2.0', '/usr/lib/python2.7/site-packages'] /home/student
```

> **Programming Humor**
>
> Definition of recursion:
>
> 1. Stop when you understand the definition.
> 2. See definition of recursion.

Summary

This chapter serves as an introduction to the Python language. As with most languages discussed in this book, Python offers many other features. The purpose of this chapter was to introduce you to the language to determine whether it might meet your software development needs.

## 11

C, C++, and Java

The purpose of this chapter is different from the last three chapters. Although the goals of Chapters 8–10 were to introduce you to new languages, the assumption in this chapter is that you already have a background coding C, C++, or Java. These languages are popular on all operating systems, including Microsoft Windows.

Instead of covering the basics of C, C++, and Java, the focus on this chapter is on topics that are related to these languages. Specifically, the goal is to provide you with information regarding the Linux operating system's impact on how you create programs in these languages.

Understanding System Libraries

A library is a file that contains compiled code (typically C or C++) that developers use to add more functionality to their programs. Normally a library includes functions and declarations that are shared with the calling program. Rarely does a library do anything on its own because the goal is to define things that will be used by the calling program.

Another program calls libraries via the `#include` statement in the source code. For example:

```
#include <stdio.h>
```

The two types of library calls are

- Static:
  - Code that is included in the program at compile time
  - Filename typically ends in `.a`
  - Makes binary larger, but doesn't require additional run-time files
- Shared:
  - Code is included at run time
  - More flexible (can change library at any time)
  - Binary code is smaller; however, missing library causes program not to execute

Managing Shared Library Files

On production machines, the task of managing shared library files is often the responsibility of the system administrator. However, on your own system you may take on this responsibility. Even if you don't, understanding the basics of how these files are managed can make you a better developer.

Usually, shared library files are stored in one of the following locations on Linux distributions:

- /lib or /lib64

- /usr/lib or /usr/lib64

- /usr/local/lib or /usr/local/lib64

If your operating system is a 32-bit distribution, expect to see the libraries under /lib, /usr/lib, and /usr/local/lib. On 64-bit platforms, the /lib64, /usr/lib/64, and /usr/local/lib64 directories are where you can expect to file libraries. You may also see file libraries under the 32-bit directories because some applications may run as 32-bit even under a 64-bit operating system. See Figure 11.1 for an example of the /lib64 directory.

```
                              root@localhost:~                        _   □   ×

 File  Edit  View  Search  Terminal  Help
[root@localhost ~]# ls /lib64 | grep ".so." | head
colord-sensors
ld-linux-x86-64.so.2
libabrt_dbus.so.0
libabrt_dbus.so.0.0.1
libabrt_gui.so.0
libabrt_gui.so.0.0.1
libabrt.so.0
libabrt.so.0.0.1
libaccountsservice.so.0
libaccountsservice.so.0.0.0
[root@localhost ~]# █
```

Figure 11.1   Shared libraries.

These shared libraries follow the naming convention of libname.so.ver. In this case, the name is a unique name for the library and ver is used to indicate the version number of this library—for example, libkpathsea.so.6.1.1.

The idea of managing shared libraries on the system is to add or remove libraries as needed. This requires access to the system as the root user because only the root user can modify the configuration files.

The primary configuration file for shared libraries is the `/etc/ld.so.conf` file. However, typically only a single line is in this file:

```
[root@localhost ~]# more /etc/ld.so.conf
include ld.so.conf.d/*.conf
```

The `include` line in this file tells the system to also use all the configuration files in the specified directory. In the case of the preceding example, that would be all the files that end in `.conf` in the `/etc/ld.so.conf.d` directory:

```
[root@localhost ~]# ls /etc/ld.so.conf.d
dyninst-x86_64.conf                libiscsi-x86_64.conf
kernel-3.10.0-327.el7.x86_64.conf  mariadb-x86_64.conf
```

A big advantage exists for using this `include` method. Suppose you create some software that requires some shared libraries. To install that software on a system, you need to tell the system where these new libraries are. Instead of having to create an installation program that modifies the primary configuration file (`/etc/ld.so.conf`), your installation program can simply copy a configuration file into the `/etc/ld.so.conf.d` directory. Conversely, the uninstall program that you create to remove the software could simply delete this file from the `/etc/ld.so.conf.d` directory.

The configuration file itself is simple. It just contains a directory in which the shared libraries are stored:

```
[root@localhost ~]# more /etc/ld.so.conf.d/libiscsi-x86_64.conf
/usr/lib64/iscsi
[root@localhost ~]# ls /usr/lib64/iscsi/
libiscsi.so.2  libiscsi.so.2.0.10900
```

To add new shared libraries to the system, you first download the libraries to the system and place them into a directory. After adding new libraries, you create a configuration file in the `/etc/ld.so.conf.d` directory and then execute the `ldconfig` command.[1] You should perform all of these tasks as the root user:

```
[root@localhost ~]# ls /usr/lib64/test
mylib.so.1
[root@localhost ~]# cat /etc/ld.so.conf.d/libtest.conf
/usr/lib64/test
[root@localhost ~]# ldconfig
```

Regular users can't successfully execute the `ldconfig` command. However, if a regular user wants to use a custom shared library, then the user can download this file into her home directory and make use of the `LD_LIBRARY_PATH` to indicate the location of custom library files:

```
[student@localhost ~]$ ls lib
mylib.so.1
[student@localhost ~]$ export LD_LIBRARY_PATH=/home/student/lib
```

---

1 No news is good news for the `ldconfig` command. No output means the command worked successfully.

Viewing Shared Library Files

You can see what shared libraries a specific command uses by using the `ldd` command as demonstrated in Listing 11.1.

Listing 11.1 **The `ldd` command**

```
[root@localhost ~]# ldd /bin/cp
        linux-vdso.so.1 =>  (0x00007ffc35df9000)
        libselinux.so.1 => /lib64/libselinux.so.1 (0x00007f93faa09000)
        libacl.so.1 => /lib64/libacl.so.1 (0x00007f93fa800000)
        libattr.so.1 => /lib64/libattr.so.1 (0x00007f93fa5fa000)
        libc.so.6 => /lib64/libc.so.6 (0x00007f93fa239000)
        libpcre.so.1 => /lib64/libpcre.so.1 (0x00007f93f9fd8000)
        liblzma.so.5 => /lib64/liblzma.so.5 (0x00007f93f9db2000)
        libdl.so.2 => /lib64/libdl.so.2 (0x00007f93f9bae000)
        /lib64/ld-linux-x86-64.so.2 (0x00007f93fac42000)
        libpthread.so.0 => /lib64/libpthread.so.0 (0x00007f93f9992000)
```

The purpose of using the `ldd` command is to troubleshoot problems with code that you are writing. This command tells you not only what libraries are being called, but specifically which directory each library is being called from. This can be extremely useful when a library is not behaving as you would expect it to behave.

Building Packages

You have successfully completed creating your software and are ready to package the software so it can be installed. The two common techniques for packaging software are by using RPM and Debian.[2] Typically, you use RPM to build packages on Red Hat–based distributions (RHEL, Fedora, CentOS, and so on) and Debian on Debian-based systems (Debian, Ubuntu, Mint, and so on).

> Note
>
> Creating a software package with RPM or Debian can be very complex. The examples provided in this chapter are very general and designed to provide an overview of how to build packages.

Building RPM Packages

To build an RPM, first install the `rpm-build` software package as demonstrated in Listing 11.2. (Note that some output of the `yum` command was removed.)

---

2 Other methods you might want to consider include APK, TGZ, and PET. For example, TGZ is when you use the `tar` command to merge all files into a single file and then the `gzip` command to compress the tar file.

Listing 11.2 **Install rpm-build**

```
[root@localhost ~]# yum -y install rpm-build
Resolving Dependencies
--> Running transaction check
---> Package rpm-build.x86_64 0:4.11.3-17.el7 will be installed
--> Processing Dependency: patch >= 2.5 for package: rpm-build-4.11.3-17.el7.x86_64
--> Processing Dependency: system-rpm-config for package: rpm-build-4.11.3-17.el7.
x86_64
--> Processing Dependency: perl(Thread::Queue) for package: rpm-build-4.11.3-17.el7.
x86_64
--> Running transaction check
---> Package patch.x86_64 0:2.7.1-8.el7 will be installed
---> Package perl-Thread-Queue.noarch 0:3.02-2.el7 will be installed
---> Package redhat-rpm-config.noarch 0:9.1.0-68.el7.centos will be installed
--> Processing Dependency: dwz >= 0.4 for package: redhat-rpm-config-9.1.0-68.el7.
centos.noarch
--> Processing Dependency: perl-srpm-macros for package: redhat-rpm-config-9.1.0-68.
el7.centos.noarch
--> Running transaction check
---> Package dwz.x86_64 0:0.11-3.el7 will be installed
---> Package perl-srpm-macros.noarch 0:1-8.el7 will be installed
--> Finished Dependency Resolution

Dependencies Resolved

Transaction Summary
================================================================================
====================================
Install  1 Package (+5 Dependent packages)

Total download size: 451 k
Installed size: 944 k
Downloading packages:
Running transaction
  Installing : patch-2.7.1-8.el7.x86_64
1/6
  Installing : dwz-0.11-3.el7.x86_64
2/6
  Installing : perl-Thread-Queue-3.02-2.el7.noarch
3/6
  Installing : perl-srpm-macros-1-8.el7.noarch
4/6
  Installing : redhat-rpm-config-9.1.0-68.el7.centos.noarch
5/6
  Installing : rpm-build-4.11.3-17.el7.x86_64
6/6
  Verifying  : redhat-rpm-config-9.1.0-68.el7.centos.noarch
```

```
1/6
  Verifying   : perl-srpm-macros-1-8.el7.noarch
2/6
  Verifying   : perl-Thread-Queue-3.02-2.el7.noarch
3/6
  Verifying   : rpm-build-4.11.3-17.el7.x86_64
4/6
  Verifying   : dwz-0.11-3.el7.x86_64
5/6
  Verifying   : patch-2.7.1-8.el7.x86_64
6/6

Installed:
  rpm-build.x86_64 0:4.11.3-17.el7

Dependency Installed:
  dwz.x86_64 0:0.11-3.el7              patch.x86_64 0:2.7.1-8.el7
perl-Thread-Queue.noarch 0:3.02-2.el7
  perl-srpm-macros.noarch 0:1-8.el7  redhat-rpm-config.noarch 0:9.1.0-68.el7.centos

Complete!
```

The next step is a bit tricky because you need to create a directory structure that contains
various files, including your software and instructions on how to install the software.
I recommend downloading the source code of a sample project and using that as a template.
For example, after downloading the source code for the dovecot package, you can expand the
source code by using the rpm command as demonstrated in Listing 11.3.[3]

Listing 11.3 **Install source RPM**

```
root@localhost ~]# rpm -ivh /tmp/dovecot-2.2.10-5.el7.src.rpm
Updating / installing...
   1:dovecot-1:2.2.10-5.el7            ################################# [100%]
[root@localhost ~]# ls rpmbuild/
SOURCES  SPECS
[root@localhost ~]# ls rpmbuild/SOURCES
dovecot-1.0.beta2-mkcert-permissions.patch  dovecot-2.2.9-nodevrand.patch
dovecot-1.0.rc7-mkcert-paths.patch          dovecot-2.2-pigeonhole-0.4.2.tar.gz
dovecot-2.0-defaultconfig.patch             dovecot.conf.5
dovecot-2.1.10-reload.patch                 dovecot.init
dovecot-2.1.10-waitonline.patch             dovecot.pam
dovecot-2.1-privatetmp.patch                dovecot.sysconfig
```

---

3 For this example, I actually break a best practice policy: don't build packages while logged in as root.
   However, I am just reviewing the basics of package building. Consider exploring the use of mock, a
   system that can be used to build RPMs using a regular user account rather than the root account.

```
dovecot-2.2.10-CVE_2014_3430.patch          dovecot.tmpfilesd
dovecot-2.2.10.tar.gz                        prestartscript
[root@localhost ~]# ls rpmbuild/SPECS
dovecot.spec
```

Your source code is stored in the SOURCES directory. The spec file is used to define how to install the software. As you can tell from the following output, this file can be quite large:

```
[root@localhost ~]# wc -l rpmbuild/SPECS/dovecot.spec
1849 rpmbuild/SPECS/dovecot.spec
```

Yes, the spec file for the dovecot package is 1,849 lines long. Not all spec files will be this large (although some will be larger). Spec files are a large topic by themselves. However, they are much like BASH shell scripts, so if you read a few existing spec files, you should be able to figure out how to create your own (or modify an existing spec file).

After your source files are in the correct directory and you have created a spec file, you can build your package using the following command:

rpmbuild -ba ~/rpmbuild/SPECS/name.spec

This command creates two new subdirectories: RPMS and SRPMS. In those directories will be your package's RPM files.

Building Debian Packages

The process of building a Debian package is very similar to building a RPM package. The following are the general steps:

1. Download source code file (typically a tar file).

2. Edit configuration files:

   - debian/changelog
   - debian/rules
   - debian/control

3. Use dpkg-buildpackage to build the package.

Exploring Java Installation and Basics

In older Linux distributions, it was rare that Java came installed by default. However, almost all distributions have Java installed as part of the typical installation process. You can see whether it is installed by using the which command and, if it is installed, use the java command to determine which version is installed:

```
[root@localhost ~]# which java
/bin/java
```

```
[root@localhost ~]# java -version
openjdk version "1.8.0_91"
OpenJDK Runtime Environment (build 1.8.0_91-b14)
OpenJDK 64-Bit Server VM (build 25.91-b14, mixed mode)
```

If Java isn't installed, you can use the `apt-get` command on Debian-based systems to install it. The package name for Java on Debian-based systems is `openjdk-X.X.X.jdk` (`X.X.X` represents the version number).

If Java isn't installed on a Red Hat–based system, you can use the `yum` command to install it. The package name for Java on Debian-based systems is `java-X.X.X-openjdk`.

Programming Humor

Real programmers count from 0!

Summary

This chapter introduced some key concepts and features of Linux that are related to programming in C, C++, and Java. You learned how library files are managed and how to package software for distribution. You should also now know how to determine whether Java is installed and, if not, how to install a version of Java.

IV

Using Git

One of the biggest headaches that developers must deal with is different versions of source code. Sometimes you just need to "go back" to a previous version of code. Maintaining these versions manually can be cumbersome and time consuming.

Compounding the problem is when multiple programmers work together on a single piece of source code. A large program can be tens of thousands of lines of code with different programmers responsible for different portions of the code.

Version control software like Git can handle the complicated task of maintaining different versions of source code.

## 12

Git Essentials

This chapter introduces you to Git, including how to install the necessary software to access Git servers where your software project will be stored.

Version Control Concepts

To understand Git and the concept of version control, looking at version control from an historical perspective is helpful. There have been three generations of version control software.

The First Generation

The first generation was very simple. Developers worked on the same physical system and "checked out" one file at a time.

This generation of version control software made use of a technique called **file locking**. When a developer checked out a file, it was locked and no other developer could edit the file. Figure 12.1 illustrates the concept of this type of version control.

Examples of first-generation version control software include Revision Control System (RCS) and Source Code Control System (SCCS).

The Second Generation

The problems with the first generation included the following:

- Only one developer can work on a file at a time. This results in a bottleneck in the development process.

- Developers have to log in directly to the system that contains the version control software.

These problems were solved in the second generation of version control software. In the second generation, files are stored on a centralized server in a repository. Developers can check out separate copies of a file. When the developer completes work on a file, the file is checked in to the repository. Figure 12.2 illustrates the concept of this type of version control.

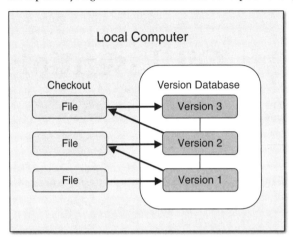

Figure 12.1   First-generation version control software

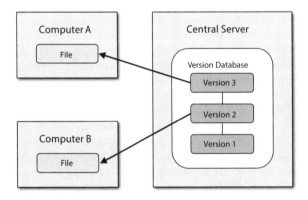

Figure 12.2   Second-generation version control software

If two developers check out the same version of a file, then the potential for issues exists. This is handled by a process called a **merge**.

What Is a Merge?

Suppose two developers, Bob and Sue, check out version 5 of a file named abc.txt. After Bob completes his work, he checks the file back in. Typically, this results in a new version of the file, version 6.

Sometime later, Sue checks in her file. This new file must incorporate her changes and Bob's changes. This is accomplished through the process of a merge.

Depending on the version control software that you use, there could be different ways to handle this merge. In some cases, such as when Bob and Sue have worked on completely different parts of the file, the merge process is very simple. However, in cases in which Sue and Bob worked on the same lines of code in the file, the merge process can be more complex. In those cases, Sue will have to make decisions, such as whether Bob's code or her code will be in the new version of the file.

After the merge process completes, the process of committing the file to the repository takes place. To commit a file essentially means to create a new version in the repository; in this case, version 7 of the file.

Examples of second-generation version control software include Concurrent Versions System (CVS) and Subversion.

The Third Generation

The third generation is referred to as Distributed Version Control Systems (DVCSs). As with the second generation, a central repository server contains all the files for the project. However, developers don't check out individual files from the repository. Instead, the entire project is checked out, allowing the developer to work on the complete set of files rather than just individual files. Figure 12.3 illustrates the concept of this type of version control.

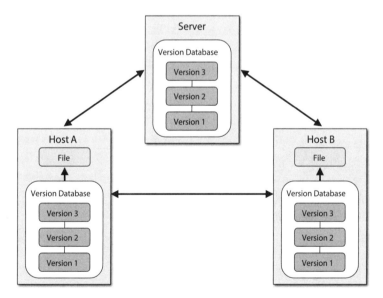

Figure 12.3   Third-generation version control software

Another (very big) difference between the second and third generation of version control software has to do with how the merge and commit process works. As previously mentioned, the steps in the second generation are to perform a merge and then commit the new version to the repository.

With third-generation version control software, files are checked in and then they are merged. To understand the difference between these two techniques, first look at Figure 12.4.

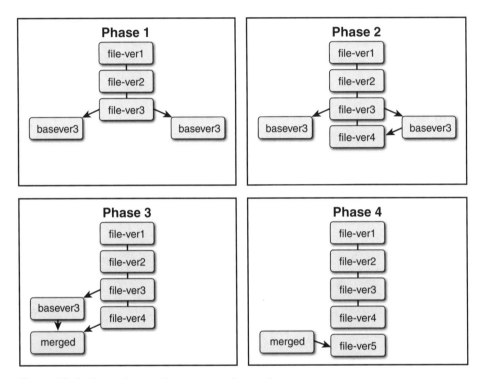

Figure 12.4   Second-generation merge and commit

In phase 1 of Figure 12.4, two developers check out a file that is based on the third version. In phase 2, one developer checks that file in, resulting in a version 4 of the file.

In phase 3 the second developer must first merge the changes from his checked-out copy with the changes of version 4 (and, potentially, other versions). After the merge is complete, the new version can be committed to the repository as version 5.

If you focus on what is in the repository (the center part of each phase), you will see that there is a very straight line of development (ver1, ver2, ver3, ver4, ver5, and so on). This simple approach to software development poses some potential problems:

- Requiring a developer to merge before committing often results in developers' not wanting to commit their changes on a regular basis. The merge process can be a pain and developers might decide to just wait until later and do one merge rather than a bunch of regular merges. This has a negative impact on software development as suddenly huge chunks of code are added to a file. Additionally, you want to encourage developers to commit changes to the repository, just like you want to encourage someone who is writing a document to save on a regular basis.

- Very important: Version 5 in this example is not necessarily the work that the developer originally completed. During the merging process, the developer might discard some of his work to complete the merge process. This isn't ideal because it results in the loss of potentially good code.

A better, although arguably more complex, technique can be employed. It is called **Directed Acyclic Graph (DAG)**, and you can see an example of how it works in Figure 12.5.

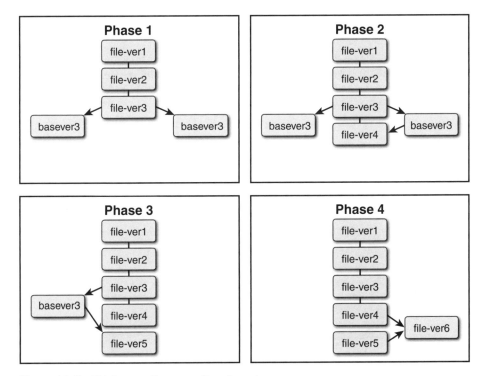

Figure 12.5   Third-generation commit and merge

Phases 1 and 2 are the same as shown in Figure 12.4. However, note that in phase 3 the second "check in" process results in a version 5 file that is not based on version 4, but rather independent of version 4. In phase 4 of the process, versions 4 and 5 of the file have been merged to create a version 6.

Although this process is more complex (and, potentially, much more complex if you have a large number of developers), it does provide some advantages over a "single line" of development:

- Developers can commit their changes on a regular basis and not have to worry about merging until a later time.

- The merging process could be delegated to a specific developer who has a better idea of the entire project or code than the other developers have.

- At any time, the project manager can go back and see exactly what work each individual developer created.

Certainly an argument exists for both methods. However, keep in mind that this book focuses on Git, which uses the Directed Acyclic Graph method of third-generation version control systems.

Installing Git

You might already have Git[1] on your system because it is sometimes installed by default (or another administrator might have installed it). If you have access to the system as a regular user, you can execute the following command to determine whether you have Git installed:

```
ocs@ubuntu:~$ which git
/usr/bin/git
```

If Git is installed, then the path to the `git` command is provided, as shown in the preceding command. If it isn't installed, then you either get no output or an error like the following:

```
[ocs@centos ~]# which git
/usr/bin/which: no git in (/usr/lib64/qt-3.3/bin:/usr/local/bin:/usr/local/sbin:/usr/
bin:/usr/sbin:/bin:/sbin:/root/bin)
```

As an administrator on a Debian-based system, you could use the `dpkg` command to determine whether the git package has been installed:

```
root@ubuntu:~# dpkg -l git
Desired=Unknown/Install/Remove/Purge/Hold
| Status=Not/Inst/Conf-files/Unpacked/halF-conf/Half-inst/trig-aWait/
➥Trig-pend
|/ Err?=(none)/Reinst-required (Status,Err: uppercase=bad)
||/ Name      Version        Architecture  Description
+++-=========-==============-============-=============================================
ii  git       1:1.9.1-1ubun  amd64         fast, scalable, distributed
➥revision con
```

---

1 When I refer to Git with a capital *I*, I am referring to the software project. When I refer to `git` with a lowercase *g* and in code font, I am referring to either the command or the software package (most often the command).

As an administrator on a Red Hat–based system, you could use the `rpm` command to determine whether the git package has been installed:

```
[root@centos ~]# rpm -q git
git-1.8.3.1-6.el7_2.1.x86_64
```

If Git isn't installed on your system, you must either log in as the root user or use `sudo` or `su` to install the software. If you are logged in as the root user on a Debian-based system, you can use the following command to install Git:

```
apt-get install git
```

If you are logged in as the root user on a Red Hat–based system, you can use the following command to install Git:

```
yum install git
```

Get More Than Git![2]

Consider installing the software package named `git-all`. This package includes some additional dependency packages that add more power to Git. Although you might not make use of these features in this introductory book, having them available when you are ready to perform more advanced Git functions will be good.

Git Concepts and Features

One of the challenges to using Git is just understanding the concepts behind it. If you don't understand the concepts, then all the commands just seem like some sort of black magic. This section focuses on the critical Git concepts as well as introduces you to some of the basic commands.

Git Stages

It is very important to remember that you "check out"[3] an entire project and that most of the work you do will be local to the system that you are working on. The files that you check out will be placed in a directory under your home directory.

To get a copy of a project from a Git repository, you use a process called **cloning**. Cloning doesn't just create a copy of all the files from the repository; it actually performs three primary functions:

- Creates a local repository of the project under the ***project_name*/.git** directory in your home directory. The files of the project in this location are considered to be "checked out" from the central repository.

---

2   It appears that all those Linux "jokes" have rubbed off on me.

3   I use parentheses around "check out" because in Git the process is really called **cloning**. However, some developers who are used to second-generation version control software are more comfortable with the term "check out." I tend to use the terms interchangeably when initially explaining the Git process.

- Creates a directory where you can directly see the files. This is called the **working area**. Changes made in the working area are not immediately version controlled.

- Creates a staging area. The staging area is designed to store changes to files before you commit them to the local repository.

This means that if you were to clone a project called Jacumba, the entire project would be stored in the `Jacumba/.git` directory under your home directory. You should not attempt to modify these directly. Instead, look directly in the `~/Jacumba` directory and you will see the files from the project. These are the files that you should change.

Suppose you made a change to a file, but you have to work on some other files before you were ready to commit changes to the local repository. In that case, you would *stage* the file that you have finished working on. This would prepare it to be committed to the local repository.

After you make all changes and stage all files, then you commit them to the local repository. See Figure 12.6 for a visual demonstration of this process.

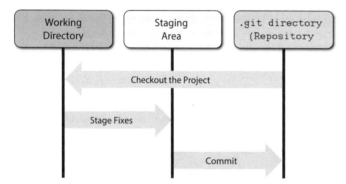

Figure 12.6   Git stages

Realize that committing the staged files only sends them to the local repository. This means that only you have access to the changes that have been made. The process of "checking in" the new versions to the central repository is called a **push**.

I explain each of these steps in greater detail later. Consider this to be an introduction to the concepts that will help you understand the process better when I introduce the Git commands.

Choosing Your Git Repository Host

First, the good news: Many organizations provide Git hosting—at the time of this writing, more than two dozen choices. This means you have many options to choose from. That's the good news...and the bad news.

It is only bad news because it means you really need to spend some time researching the pros and cons of the different hosting organizations. For example, most don't charge for basic hosting but do charge for large-scale projects. Some only provide public repositories (anyone can see your repository) whereas others allow you to create private repositories. There are many other features to consider.

One of the features that might be high on your list is a web interface. Although you can do just about all repository operations locally on your system, being able to perform some operations via a web interface can be very useful. Explore the interface that is provided before making your choice.

Consider This

I am not going to make a suggestion regarding which Git host you should use because it really does vary based on what your needs are. Many websites provide up-to-date comparisons between the various Git hosts, and I strongly recommend you do your homework before deciding on one.

At the very least, I recommend considering the following:

- https://bitbucket.org
- http://www.cloudforge.com
- http://www.codebasehq.com
- https://github.com
- http://gitlab.com

Note that I chose gitlab.com for the examples in the book. Any of the hosts in the preceding list would have been just fine for the book; I just chose gitlab.com because it happened to be the one I used on my last Git project.

Configuring Git

Now that you have gotten through all the theory,[4] it is time to actually do something with Git. This next section assumes the following:

- You have installed the `git` or `git-all` software package on your system.
- You have created an account on a Git hosting service.

The first thing you want to do is perform some basic setup. Whenever you perform a commit operation, your name and email address will be included in the metadata. To set this information, execute the following commands:

```
ocs@ubuntu:~$ git config --global user.name "Bo Rothwell"
ocs@ubuntu:~$ git config --global user.email "bo@onecoursesource.com"
```

---

4 Trust me, the theory will help a lot!

Obviously you will replace `"Bo Rothwell"` with your name and `"bo@OneCourseSource.com"` with your email address. The next step is to clone your project from the Git hosting service. Note that before cloning, only one file is in the user's home directory:

```
ocs@ubuntu:~$ ls
first.sh
```

The following cloned a project named ocs:

```
ocs@ubuntu:~$ git clone https://gitlab.com/borothwell/ocs.git
Cloning into 'ocs'...
Username for 'https://gitlab.com': borothwell
Password for 'https://borothwell@gitlab.com':
remote: Counting objects: 3, done.
remote: Total 3 (delta 0), reused 0 (delta 0)
Unpacking objects: 100% (3/3), done.
Checking connectivity... done.
```

After successful execution, notice a new directory in the user's home directory:

```
ocs@ubuntu:~$ ls
first.sh  ocs
```

If you switch to the new directory, you can see what was cloned from the repository (only one file so far exists in the repository):

```
ocs@ubuntu:~$ cd ocs
ocs@ubuntu:~/ocs$ ls
README.md
```

Next, create a new file in the repository directory. You can either create one from scratch or copy a file from another location:

```
ocs@ubuntu:~/ocs$ cp ../first.sh
```

Remember, anything placed in this directory is not version controlled because this is the working directory. To put it in the local repository, you first have to add it to the staging area and then you need to commit it to the repository:

```
ocs@ubuntu:~/ocs$ git add first.sh
ocs@ubuntu:~/ocs$ git commit -m "added first.sh"
[master 3b36054] added first.sh
1 file changed, 5 insertions(+)
create mode 100644 first.sh
```

The `git add` command places the file in the staging area. The `git commit` command takes all the new files in the staging area and commits them to the local repository. You use the `-m` option to add a message; in this case the reason for the commit was given.

It is important to highlight that no changes have been made to the repository on the server. The `git commit` command only updates the local repository. You can see that the server repository has not been modified by looking at Figure 12.7, which shows a screenshot of the web-based interface of the current project. Notice that the original file, `README.md`, was pushed to the server several days ago, but the new file, `first.sh`, does not have an entry.

Figure 12.7   Server repository is unchanged after executing the git commit command

Most likely you would make additional changes to your local project and then "check in" (push) the changes to the server's repository:

```
ocs@ubuntu:~/ocs$ git push -u origin master
Username for 'https://gitlab.com': borothwell
Password for 'https://borothwell@gitlab.com':
Counting objects: 4, done.
Compressing objects: 100% (3/3), done.
Writing objects: 100% (3/3), 370 bytes | 0 bytes/s, done.
Total 3 (delta 0), reused 0 (delta 0)
To https://gitlab.com/borothwell/ocs.git
   12424f5..3b36054  master -> master
Branch master set up to track remote branch master from origin.
```

See Figure 12.8 to verify the push was successful.

Figure 12.8   Server repository is changed after executing the git push command

At this point all changes of the files from the staging area have been updated to the local repository and the central server repository.

> **Git Humor**
>
> Wiser words may have never been spoken: "Commit early, commit often. A tip for version controlling—not for relationships."
>
> —Anonymous

Summary

This chapter focused on the key concepts of Git. You should now understand the concepts of version control in addition to specifics about how to perform version control with Git.

## 13

Manage Files with Git

Git provides a rich collection of features, but the core set of features are the ones that you are going to use the most often. This includes commands that enable you to stage files and commit files to the local repository, as well as create branches. This chapter focuses on these topics as well as a few related ones.

Basic Configuration

You might want to perform several configuration operations. For example, you can set your default editor by executing the following command:

```
ocs@ubuntu:~/ocs$ git config --global core.editor vi
```

You can view current configuration settings by executing the `git config --list` command:

```
ocs@ubuntu:~/ocs$ git config --list
user.name=Bo Rothwell
user.email=bo@onecoursesource.com
core.editor=editor_name
core.repositoryformatversion=0
core.filemode=true
core.bare=false
core.logallrefupdates=true
remote.origin.url=https://gitlab.com/borothwell/ocs.git
remote.origin.fetch=+refs/heads/*:refs/remotes/origin/*
branch.master.remote=origin
branch.master.merge=refs/heads/master
```

You can store configuration information in multiple locations. One location is in your own home directory:

```
ocs@ubuntu:~/ocs$ more ~/.gitconfig
[user]
        name = Bo Rothwell
        email = bo@onecoursesource.com
[core]
        editor = vi
```

An administrator can also store configuration information for all users in the `/etc/gitconfig` file. The additional settings that you see when you execute the `git config --list` command are either default settings or are derived from the information in the local repository.

> **Getting Help**
>
> Besides looking at man pages for information about `git` commands, you might consider the `git help` command. When run with no additional arguments, the `git help` command provides a synopsis of how the command should be executed followed by a summary of `git` commands (`config`, `add`, `clone`, `commit`, `push`, and so on).
>
> To see information about a specific command, execute `git help` *command*. For example: `git help config`. This automatically puts you in the man page for that command.

git status

In Chapter 12, "Git Essentials," you learned how to clone an existing repository from a central repository server. You also learned the lifecycle of how local files are committed to the local repository and then pushed to the central repository server:

1. Create the file in the repository directory.

2. Add the file to the staging area with the `git add` command.

3. Commit the file to the repository with the `git commit` command.

4. Push the file to the central server with the `git push` command.

> **Note**
>
> You can combine the `git add` and `git commit` commands into a single operation by using the `-a` option to the `git commit` command.

Imagine you are working on some files one day and it's getting late. It is Friday afternoon and you just can't wait for the weekend to start. On the following Monday you arrive at work and realize you have no idea in what area you left your file. Were they added to the staging area? All of them or just some? Did you commit any of them to the local repository?

This is when you want to run the `git status` command:

```
ocs@ubuntu:~/ocs$ git status
On branch master
Your branch is up-to-date with 'origin/master'.

nothing to commit, working directory clean
```

> **Note**
>
> It makes a difference which directory you are in when you execute the `git status` command. For example, if you are in your home directory, all the files in this directory will be checked to see whether they are in the repository:
>
> ```
> ocs@ubuntu:~$ git status
> On branch master
>
>
> Initial commit
>
>
> Untracked files:
>   (use "git add <file>..." to include in what will be committed)
>
>
>   .bash_history
>   .bash_logout
>   .bashrc
>   .gitconfig
>   .lesshst
>   .profile
>   .viminfo
>   ocs/
>
>
> nothing added to commit but untracked files present (use "git add"
> ➥to track)
> ```
>
> Make sure you are in the repository directory before running this command!

If you make changes to a file and don't add it to the staging area, then the output of the `git status` command will look like the following:

```
ocs@ubuntu:~/ocs$ git status
On branch master
Your branch is up-to-date with 'origin/master'.

Changes not staged for commit:
  (use "git add <file>..." to update what will be committed)
  (use "git checkout -- <file>..." to discard changes in working directory)

        modified:   first.sh

no changes added to commit (use "git add" and/or "git commit -a")
```

Notice in the previous output the `Changes not staged for commit` section. The command output also is helpful in showing you how you can stage the command with the `git add` command or stage and commit with the `git commit -a` command.

If a file has been added to the staging area, but not committed to the local repository, then the output of the `git status` command will look like the following:

```
ocs@ubuntu:~/ocs$ git add first.sh
ocs@ubuntu:~/ocs$ git status
On branch master
Your branch is up-to-date with 'origin/master'.

Changes to be committed:
  (use "git reset HEAD <file>..." to unstage)

       modified:   first.sh
```

`Changes to be committed` means the modified file is in the staging area but not in the local repository. If a file has been committed to local repository, but not committed to the central repository server, then the output of the `git status` command will look like the following:

```
ocs@ubuntu:~/ocs$ git commit -m "demostrating status"
[master 9eb721e] demostrating status
 1 file changed, 2 insertions(+), 1 deletion(-)
ocs@ubuntu:~/ocs$ git status
On branch master
Your branch is ahead of 'origin/master' by 1 commit.
  (use "git push" to publish your local commits)

nothing to commit, working directory clean
```

Note that `nothing to commit, working directory clean` means the staging area no longer contains any files and the working directory reflects the current contents of the local repository. Also note the message that states `Your branch is ahead of 'origin/master' by 1 commit`. This makes it clear that you need to execute `git push` to push the contents of the local repository to the central repository server.

Executing the `git status` command after successfully executing the `git push` command results in the output demonstrated in the original example of this chapter as shown in Listing 13.1.

Listing 13.1 **All files up to date**

```
ocs@ubuntu:~/ocs$ git push -u origin master
Username for 'https://gitlab.com': borothwell
Password for 'https://borothwell@gitlab.com':
Counting objects: 5, done.
Compressing objects: 100% (3/3), done.
Writing objects: 100% (3/3), 381 bytes | 0 bytes/s, done.
Total 3 (delta 0), reused 0 (delta 0)
```

```
To https://gitlab.com/borothwell/ocs.git
   3b36054..9eb721e  master -> master
Branch master set up to track remote branch master from origin.
ocs@ubuntu:~/ocs$ git status
On branch master
Your branch is up-to-date with 'origin/master'.

nothing to commit, working directory clean
```

Handling a Multiple Location Situation

Because of the staging area, the possibility exists to have one version of the file in the local repository, a second version in the staging area, and a third in the working directory. This can happen after you edit a file, add it to the staging area, and then edit the file again. When this happens, the output of the git status command will look like that shown in Listing 13.2.

Listing 13.2   **Three versions of a file**

```
ocs@ubuntu:~/ocs$ git status
On branch master
Your branch is up-to-date with 'origin/master'.

Changes to be committed:
  (use "git reset HEAD <file>..." to unstage)

      modified:   first.sh

Changes not staged for commit:
  (use "git add <file>..." to update what will be committed)
  (use "git checkout -- <file>..." to discard changes in working
➥directory)

      modified:   first.sh
```

In the output of Listing 13.2, you can see that the first.sh file is listed both as Changes to be committed and Changes not staged for commit. Now you must make a choice:

- **Commit both versions of the file**—First execute the git commit command, then execute git add, and then execute git commit again.

- **Commit the last version of the file**—First execute git add and then execute git commit.[1]

---

1 The resulting output of this git commit command tends to cause confusion: 1 file changed, 2 insertions(+), 1 deletion(-). Because two versions of the file were staged (two insertions), one had to be deleted before the other was committed to the repository.

A useful option to the `git status` command is the `-s` option, which shows a much more condensed output:

```
ocs@ubuntu:~/ocs$ git status -s
M first.sh
A  showmine.sh
?? hidden.sh
```

Each file is preceded by up to two characters. The first character indicates the status in the staging area and the second character indicates the status in the working directory. The `first. sh` file has been modified in the working directory, but you can tell that it has not been staged yet because of the space character in front of the "M" character. Note the difference if the file is staged:

```
ocs@ubuntu:~/ocs$ git add first.sh
ocs@ubuntu:~/ocs$ git status -s
M  first.sh
A  showmine.sh
?? hidden.sh
```

The `A` for the `showmine.sh` file means this is a new file that has been staged (because the `A` is in the first column), but it hasn't been committed to the repository yet. The `??` means that `hidden.sh` is new and hasn't been staged or committed yet. Any file that is up to date in the local repository is not listed when you execute the `git status -s` command.

Telling Git to Ignore a File

In some cases, you want to have a file in the working directory but not have it ever staged or placed in the repository. For example, maybe you want to keep track of some notes about the project, but only for your own purposes. Of course, you could just never add this file to the staging area, but this would mean that `git status` will never return `nothing to commit, working directory clean`.

To have `git` commands ignore a file, create a file named `.gitignore` in the working directory and place the filename to ignore inside of this file:

```
ocs@ubuntu:~/ocs$ touch notes
ocs@ubuntu:~/ocs$ git status -s
?? notes
ocs@ubuntu:~/ocs$ vi .gitignore      #added notes as shown below:
ocs@ubuntu:~/ocs$ cat .gitignore
notes
ocs@ubuntu:~/ocs$ git status -s
?? .gitignore
```

Notice that you must also place the `.gitignore` file itself in the `.gitignore` file:

```
ocs@ubuntu:~/ocs$ git status -s
?? .gitignore
ocs@ubuntu:~/ocs$ vi .gitignore      #added .gitignore as shown below:
```

```
ocs@ubuntu:~/ocs$ cat .gitignore
notes
.gitignore
ocs@ubuntu:~/ocs$ git status -s
```

Note

You can also use wildcard characters (*, ?, and [range]) in the `.gitignore` file to match a collection of files. For example, I like to name my own files with a `.me` extension. In the `.gitignore` file I include the pattern `*.me` to have the `git` commands ignore all of my files.

You can use a pattern that ends with a / to indicate an entire directory.

If You Are Following Along...

I've tried to make this process as transparent as possible, but there are some cases in which I am going to be executing some commands that don't show up in the body of the text. For example, at this point I have added several versions of the `first.sh` file (as well as two new files: the `showmine.sh` and `hidden.sh` files) to the local repository. I want to use these in later examples, so I decided to push them to the central repository server:

```
ocs@ubuntu:~/ocs$ git push -u origin master
Username for 'https://gitlab.com': borothwell
Password for 'https://borothwell@gitlab.com':
Counting objects: 10, done.
Compressing objects: 100% (7/7), done.
Writing objects: 100% (8/8), 865 bytes | 0 bytes/s, done.
Total 8 (delta 1), reused 0 (delta 0)
To https://gitlab.com/borothwell/ocs.git
   9eb721e..07bb91c  master -> master
Branch master set up to track remote branch master from origin.
```

However, this isn't critical to the topic at hand, so I opted not to show this in the main text. In the future, if I do some "behind the scenes" commands, I will mention the commands that I executed in a footnote. That way if you are following along, you should end up with the same results that I do.

Removing Files

Suppose one day you create a file purely for testing purposes and then, without really thinking about it, you commit it to the local repository:[2]

```
ocs@ubuntu:~/ocs$ git add test.sh
ocs@ubuntu:~/ocs$ git commit "update 27"
```

Later, you realize your mistake and want to remove the file. Simply removing it from the working directory isn't enough, as demonstrated in Listing 13.3.[3]

Listing 13.3   **Deleting file from working directory**

```
ocs@ubuntu:~/ocs$ rm test.sh
ocs@ubuntu:~/ocs$ git status
On branch master
Your branch is ahead of 'origin/master' by 1 commit.
  (use "git push" to publish your local commits)

Changes not staged for commit:
  (use "git add/rm <file>..." to update what will be committed)
  (use "git checkout -- <file>..." to discard changes in working directory)

        deleted:    test.sh

no changes added to commit (use "git add" and/or "git commit -a")
```

Notice the suggestion to execute the `git rm` command, which will stage the file for removal from the repository. See Listing 13.4 for an example of the `git rm` command.

Listing 13.4   **Staging a file to be deleted**

```
ocs@ubuntu:~/ocs$ git rm test.sh
rm 'test.sh'
ocs@ubuntu:~/ocs$ git status
On branch master
Your branch is ahead of 'origin/master' by 1 commit.
  (use "git push" to publish your local commits)

Changes to be committed:
  (use "git reset HEAD <file>..." to unstage)

        deleted:    test.sh
```

---

2   This potential mistake might be the reason why you must execute `git add` and then `git commit` for new files (you can't just execute `git commit -a` to add a new file).

3   However, nothing is wrong with executing a regular `rm` command because you probably want to delete this file from the working directory. This just isn't going to end up removing it from the repository.

Lastly, perform a `git commit` command to remove the file from the repository:

```
ocs@ubuntu:~/ocs$ git commit -m "deleting test.sh file"
[master 2b44792] deleting test.sh file
 1 file changed, 1 deletions(-)
 delete mode 100644 test.sh
```

Handling Branches

You decide that you want to test some new features of the project that you are working on, but you don't want this to impact the current development process. This is an ideal time to create a branch.

When you first create a project, the code is associated with a branch called `master`. If you want to create a new branch, execute the `git branch` command:

```
ocs@ubuntu:~/ocs$ git branch test
```

This doesn't mean you are suddenly working in the new branch. As you can see from the output of the `git status` command, the `git branch` command doesn't change your current branch:

```
ocs@ubuntu:~/ocs$ git status
On branch master
Your branch is ahead of 'origin/master' by 2 commits.
  (use "git push" to publish your local commits)

nothing to commit, working directory clean
```

The first line of the output of the previous command, `On branch master` denotes that you are still working in the `master` branch. To switch to the new branch, execute the `git checkout` command:[4]

```
ocs@ubuntu:~/ocs$ git checkout test
Switched to branch 'test'
```

Switching actually does two things:

- Makes it so any future commits occur on the `test` branch
- Makes it so the working directory reflects the `test` branch

The second item makes more sense with a demonstration. First, observe the following commands, which will end up with a new version of the `hidden.sh` file being placed in the `test` branch repository:

---

4 You can create a branch and switch to it by using the `-b` option to the `git checkout` command:
   `git checkout -b test`

```
ocs@ubuntu:~/ocs$ git add hidden.sh
ocs@ubuntu:~/ocs$ git commit -m "changed hidden.sh"
[test ef2d7d5] changed hidden.sh
1 file changed, 1 insertion(+)
```

Note what the file looks like in the current working directory:

```
ocs@ubuntu:~/ocs$ more hidden.sh
#!/bin/bash
#hidden.sh

echo "Listing only hidden files:"
ls -ld .* $1
```

If we switch the project back to the master branch, you can see how the hidden.sh file in the working directory is different (note the missing echo line, which was added for the test branch only):

```
ocs@ubuntu:~/ocs$ git checkout master
Switched to branch 'master'
Your branch is ahead of 'origin/master' by 2 commits.
  (use "git push" to publish your local commits)
ocs@ubuntu:~/ocs$ more hidden.sh
#!/bin/bash
#hidden.sh
ls -ld .* $1
```

You can see the changes that are made on different branches, along with the comments you provided for each change, by using the git log command:

```
ocs@ubuntu:~/ocs$ git log --oneline --decorate --all
ef2d7d5 (test) changed hidden.sh
2b44792 (HEAD, master) deleting test.sh file
19198d7 update 27
07bb91c (origin/master, origin/HEAD) adding showmine.sh and hidden.sh
75d717b added first.sh
9eb721e demostrating status5
3b36054 added first.sh
12424f5 add README
```

The--online option has the git log command provide a one-line summary of each change. The--decorate option requests additional information such as the branch name. The--all option asks to see the log for all branches, not just the current branch.

---

5 Just a side note for those of you paying close attention: the spelling error (demostrating, when it should be demonstrating) is actually how the output of the command was displayed.

Pushing Branches

Recall the command to push changes to the central repository server:

```
git push -u origin master
```

Did you wonder at the time what the word *master* meant? You can probably guess now that it was the branch that you were pushing to the central repository. If you wanted to push the test branch, then you would have to execute the following command as well:[6]

```
git push -u origin test
```

There is more to the story of branching besides just creating a branch and switching back and forth between branches. For example, at some point you might want to merge files from branches together. You might also want to see how versions of files are different between different branches. Chapter 14, "Manage Differences in Files" covers these topics.

> **Git Humor**
>
> "Be careful not to remove the branch you're standing on."
>
> —Anonymous

Summary

After reading this chapter, you should have a firm understanding of how the working directory, staging area, and local repository work. You should also know how to determine which of these locations a file is currently "in" as well as how to specify files that the git commands should ignore. You should understand the basics of branching, including how to create branches, switch between branches, add/commit in different branches, and push different branches to the central repository server.

---

6 If are following along, you should know that I did execute both `git push` commands to update the master and test branch. I use this data in Chapter 14 examples.

## 14

Manage Differences in Files

Typically, developers love writing code. Unfortunately, writing code is not the only responsibility of software developers. Searching for differences between two versions of source code files and merging them into a new version is a major part of writing code.

The Git software tries to make this process easier by providing you with tools that display the difference between files and help you merge files together. These tools are the focus of this chapter.

Executing Diffs

You arrive at work Monday morning, ready to start on your project. Executing the `git status` command when you haven't worked on the project for a while is always a good habit, so you execute the command and discover that you have a file in the working area that hasn't been staged:

```
ocs@ubuntu:~/ocs$ git status
On branch master
Your branch is up-to-date with 'origin/master'.

Changes not staged for commit:
  (use "git add <file>..." to update what will be committed)
  (use "git checkout -- <file>..." to discard changes in working directory)

      modified:   hidden.sh

no changes added to commit (use "git add" and/or "git commit -a")
```

You could just stage and commit the file, but you wonder what changes were made to this file. Maybe you didn't finish making the changes last Friday. This might pose problems, so comparing the version of the file in the working directory with the version that has most recently been committed to the local repository is best. You can do this by executing the `git diff` command:

```
ocs@ubuntu:~/ocs$ git diff hidden.sh | cat -n
     1  diff --git a/hidden.sh b/hidden.sh
     2  index 05151ce..714482b 100644
     3  --- a/hidden.sh
```

```
 4  +++ b/hidden.sh
 5  @@ -1,4 +1,5 @@
 6   #!/bin/bash
 7   #hidden.sh
 8
 9  +echo "Hidden files:"
10   ls -ld .* $1
```

The output of this command requires a bit of explaining.[1] Ignore the first two lines of output because they aren't important at this point.

Lines 3 and 4 refer to the two versions of the file. Each version is assigned a letter (a or b) to distinguish between the two. Line 3 refers to the version that has been committed, whereas line 4 refers to the version in the working directory.

Line 5 gives "directions" on how to make the two files look the same. In this case, it is simply saying "at line 4 of the 'a' file add line 5 of the 'b' file." Following these directions would make the files look the same by making the committed version look like the version in the working directory.

Lines 6–10 visually show what changes would have to take place in the committed version to make it look like the version in the working directory. A + before a line means "add this" and a – before a line means "remove this."

> **Note**
>
> The output of the `git diff` command is referred to as **patch** output. You can use this output to patch a file (essentially, upgrade the file to the most current version). Chapter 15, "Advanced Git Features" covers this process.

Understanding that this comparison is performed on a line-by-line basis is important. A single change on one line would mean the lines are completely different to the `git diff` command. For example, look at Listing 14.1 and notice that the only difference between lines 9 and 11 is a single character.

Listing 14.1 **A single difference**

```
ocs@ubuntu:~/ocs$ git diff hidden.sh | cat -n
     1  diff --git a/hidden.sh b/hidden.sh
     2  index 05151ce..6de92ae 100644
     3  --- a/hidden.sh
     4  +++ b/hidden.sh
     5  @@ -1,4 +1,5 @@
     6   #!/bin/bash
     7   #hidden.sh
     8
```

---

1 If you run this on your own system and don't pipe the output to the `cat` command, you should see some color highlight that helps you understand the data.

```
 9  -ls -ld .* $1
10  +echo "Hidden files:"
11  +ls -ldh .* $1
```

By default, the `git diff` command compares versions in the following two situations:

- If the working directory version is different than the committed version, but only if the working version hasn't been staged

- If the working directory version is different than the staged version

That means if you stage a file, the `git diff` command won't compare the staged version to the committed version, at least not by default. As you can see, there is no output for the following `git diff` command:

```
ocs@ubuntu:~/ocs$ git add hidden.sh
ocs@ubuntu:~/ocs$ git diff | cat -n
```

To compare a staged version to a committed version, use the `--staged` option as shown in Listing 14.2.

Listing 14.2 **Staged versus committed difference**

```
ocs@ubuntu:~/ocs$ git diff --staged hidden.sh | cat -n
     1  diff --git a/hidden.sh b/hidden.sh
     2  index 05151ce..6de92ae 100644
     3  --- a/hidden.sh
     4  +++ b/hidden.sh
     5  @@ -1,4 +1,5 @@
     6   #!/bin/bash
     7   #hidden.sh
     8
     9  -ls -ld .* $1
    10  +echo "Hidden files:"
    11  +ls -ldh .* $1
```

Dealing with White Space

A useful option to the `git diff` command is the `--check` option, which looks for white spaces. To understand the importance of this, first look at the output of Listing 14.3.

Listing 14.3 **White space mystery**

```
ocs@ubuntu:~/ocs$ git diff --staged  hidden.sh | cat -n
     1  diff --git a/hidden.sh b/hidden.sh
     2  index 6de92ae..519eb3c 100644
     3  --- a/hidden.sh
     4  +++ b/hidden.sh
```

```
 5  @@ -1,5 +1,5 @@
 6   #!/bin/bash
 7  -#hidden.sh
 8  +#hidden.sh
 9
10   echo "Hidden files:"
11   ls -ldh .* $1
```

Based on the output of Listing 14.3, lines 7 and 8 are different. However, they look exactly the same. To see why they are different use the `--check` option:

```
ocs@ubuntu:~/ocs$ git diff --staged --check | cat -n
     1  hidden.sh:2: trailing whitespace.
     2  +#hidden.sh
```

The message `trailing whitespace` means some sort of white space characters (spaces, tabs, and so on) are at the end of the line.[2]

Comparing Branches

You can also use the `git diff` command to compare files in different branches. For example, to see a list of files that are different between two branches, use the following command:

```
ocs@ubuntu:~/ocs$ git diff --name-status master..test
M       hidden.sh
```

In the previous `git diff` command, the `--name-status` option provides a summary of the files that are different in the two branches. The two branches, `master` and `test`, are listed, separated by `..` characters.

To see the differences between the versions in the two branches, use the syntax shown in Listing 14.4.

Listing 14.4 `git diff` between branches

```
ocs@ubuntu:~/ocs$ git diff master:hidden.sh test:hidden.sh
diff --git a/master:hidden.sh b/test:hidden.sh
index 519eb3c..804fcf7 100644
--- a/master:hidden.sh
+++ b/test:hidden.sh
@@ -1,5 +1,5 @@
 #!/bin/bash
-#hidden.sh
+#hidden.sh

-echo "Hidden files:"
-ls -ldh .* $1
+echo "Listing only hidden files:"
+ls -ld .* $1
```

---

2 Note that I executed `git commit` at this point.

If you find the output of the `git diff` command to be confusing, consider using the `git difftool` command:[3]

```
ocs@ubuntu:~/ocs$ git difftool hidden.sh

This message is displayed because 'diff.tool' is not configured.
See 'git difftool --tool-help' or 'git help config' for more details.
'git difftool' will now attempt to use one of the following tools:
opendiff kdiff3 tkdiff xxdiff meld kompare gvimdiff diffuse diffmerge ecmerge p4merge
araxis bc3 codecompare emerge vimdiff

Viewing (1/1): 'hidden.sh'
Launch 'vimdiff' [Y/n]: y
2 files to edit
```

Note how it prompts you for the tool to use to display the differences. It also lists the tools that could be available.[4] If you want to use a different tool than the one it chooses, then execute the command as shown in the following:

```
git difftool --tool=<tool> file
```

The output of `git difftool` appears in a more readable format. For example, see Figure 14.1 for the output of `git difftool` when you use the `vimdiff` command as the display tool.[5]

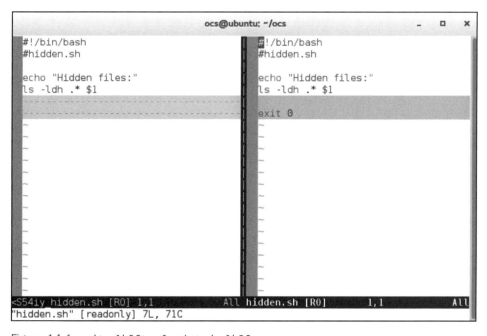

Figure 14.1   `git difftool` using `vimdiff`

---

3 Note that you need to install the `git-all` package if you want to use the `git difftool` command.

4 Most likely not all of these tools are installed on your system.

5 Note that I executed `git commit` at this point.

Merging Files

Suppose you create a new branch to add a new feature to a file as demonstrated in Listing 14.5.

Listing 14.5   **Features branch**

```
ocs@ubuntu:~/ocs$ more showmine.sh
#!/bin/bash
#showmine.sh

echo "Your processes:"
ps -fe | grep $USER | more
ocs@ubuntu:~/ocs$ git checkout -b feature127
Switched to a new branch 'feature127'
ocs@ubuntu:~/ocs$ vi showmine.sh
ocs@ubuntu:~/ocs$ more showmine.sh
#!/bin/bash
#showmine.sh

echo -n "Enter name username or press enter: "
read person

echo "${person:-$USER} processes:"
ps -fe | grep "^${person:-$USER}" | more
```

After testing out this new feature (look at the last two lines of the output of Listing 14.5 to see the new feature), you are ready to implement it in the master branch. To do this, you will need to merge the content from the feature127 branch into the master branch. Start by committing all changes in the feature127 branch and then switch back to the master branch:

```
ocs@ubuntu:~/ocs$ git commit -a -m "feature added to showmine.sh"
[feature127 2e5defa] feature added to showmine.sh
 1 file changed, 5 insertions(+), 2 deletions(-)
ocs@ubuntu:~/ocs$ git checkout master
Switched to branch 'master'
Your branch is ahead of 'origin/master' by 3 commits.
  (use "git push" to publish your local commits)
```

You must be in the branch that you want to merge into in order to correctly run the next command. The following git merge command merges the changes from the feature127 branch into the master branch:

```
ocs@ubuntu:~/ocs$ git merge feature127
Updating 4810ca8..2e5defa
Fast-forward
 showmine.sh | 7 +++++--
 1 file changed, 5 insertions(+), 2 deletions(-)
```

After the feature has been implemented, you may decide that the feature127 branch is no longer necessary. To remove this branch, execute the following command:

```
ocs@ubuntu:~/ocs$ git branch -d feature127
Deleted branch feature127 (was 2e5defa).
```

This merge process can be more complex. For example, there was a separate branch named test that was branched off an earlier version of the master branch. In the test branch, the most recent showmine.sh script looks like the following:

```
ocs@ubuntu:~/ocs$ git checkout test
ocs@ubuntu:~/ocs$ more showmine.sh
#!/bin/bash
#showmine.sh

echo "Your programs:"
ps -fe | grep $USER | more

echo -n "Enter a PID to stop: "
read proc
kill $proc
```

The current version of showmine.sh that has been committed to the master branch looks like the following:

```
ocs@ubuntu:~/ocs$ git checkout master
Switched to branch 'master'
Your branch is ahead of 'origin/master' by 4 commits.
  (use "git push" to publish your local commits)
ocs@ubuntu:~/ocs$ more showmine.sh
#!/bin/bash
#showmine.sh

echo -n "Enter name username or press enter: "
read person

echo "${person:-$USER} processes:"
ps -fe | grep "^${person:-$USER}" | more
```

Should you merge the changes from the master into the test branch? Or should you merge the changes from the test branch into the master branch? Typically, if you have more work to do in the test branch, merge the changes from the master into the test branch. Otherwise, merge the changes from the test branch into the master branch.

The following example merges the changes from the master branch into the test branch:

```
ocs@ubuntu:~/ocs$ git checkout test
Switched to branch 'test'
Your branch is ahead of 'origin/test' by 1 commit.
  (use "git push" to publish your local commits)
```

```
ocs@ubuntu:~/ocs$ git merge master
Auto-merging showmine.sh
CONFLICT (content): Merge conflict in showmine.sh
Auto-merging hidden.sh
CONFLICT (content): Merge conflict in hidden.sh
Automatic merge failed; fix conflicts and then commit the result.
```

You can see that the merge was not completed because the automated merge process ran into some conflicts. You can also see these conflicts by executing the git status command:

```
ocs@ubuntu:~/ocs$ git status
On branch test
Your branch is ahead of 'origin/test' by 1 commit.
  (use "git push" to publish your local commits)

You have unmerged paths.
  (fix conflicts and run "git commit")

Unmerged paths:
  (use "git add <file>..." to mark resolution)

        both modified:      hidden.sh
        both modified:      showmine.sh

no changes added to commit (use "git add" and/or "git commit -a")
```

This makes it clearer that two files have conflicts, not just one. If you look at the new showmine.sh file in the working directory, it will look something like Listing 14.6.

Listing 14.6   **Merged file**

```
ocs@ubuntu:~/ocs$ cat -n showmine.sh
     1  #!/bin/bash
     2  #showmine.sh
     3
     4  <<<<<<< HEAD
     5  echo "Your programs:"
     6  ps -fe | grep $USER | more
     7
     8  echo -n "Enter a PID to stop: "
     9  read proc
    10  kill $proc
    11
    12  =======
    13  echo -n "Enter name username or press enter: "
    14  read person
    15
    16  echo "${person:-$USER} processes:"
    17  ps -fe | grep "^${person:-$USER}" | more
    18  >>>>>>> master
```

Essentially, the file contains the contents of each file. Rather than try to edit this file directly, one way to handle these conflicts is to use the `git mergetool` command:[6]

```
ocs@ubuntu:~/ocs$ git mergetool showmine.sh

This message is displayed because 'merge.tool' is not configured.
See 'git mergetool --tool-help' or 'git help config' for more details.
'git mergetool' will now attempt to use one of the following tools:
opendiff kdiff3 tkdiff xxdiff meld tortoisemerge gvimdiff diffuse diffmerge ecmerge
p4merge araxis bc3 codecompare emerge vimdiff
Merging:
showmine.sh

Normal merge conflict for 'showmine.sh':
  {local}: modified file
  {remote}: modified file
Hit return to start merge resolution tool (vimdiff):
```

The `git mergetool` command displays the files using one of the diff tools. For example, using the `vimdiff` tool displays as shown in Figure 14.2.[7]

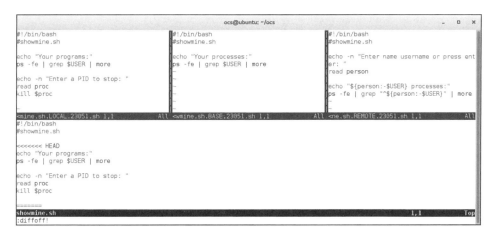

Figure 14.2   `git mergetool` using `vimdiff`

The first time you see this output, you might be a bit overwhelmed. It isn't as bad as you might think. To see how this works, look at Figure 14.3.

---

6 Note that you need to install the `git-all` package if you want to use the `git mergetool` command.

7 The `vimdiff` utility highlights differences using colors that are sure to give you a headache if you look at them too long. I highly suggest executing the `:diffoff!` command immediately to avoid visual problems and dizziness. However, when you want to make changes to the file, you need to turn this feature back on by executing the `:window diffthis` command.

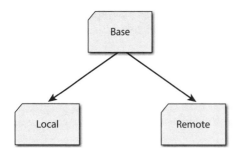

Figure 14.3   Understanding `vimdiff`

BASE is what the file looked like when the two branches were last in sync. LOCAL represents how the file looks in the current branch (the `test` branch in this example). REMOTE represents how the file looks like in the branch that is being merged into this branch (the `master` branch in this example). The file at the bottom is the file that you are creating/merging.

As you can see from Figure 14.2, the first three lines of all versions of the file are identical. If you go to the first line that differs between the LOCAL and REMOTE, you can execute the `:diffget RE` command to grab the code from the REMOTE file. This would grab the `echo`, `read`, `echo`, and `ps` commands in this example.

Suppose you want to input specific lines from one of the three files? For example, you want to copy the last four lines of the LOCAL version into the merged area. In this case you essentially do a copy and paste operation.

To switch to the LOCAL window, hold down the Ctrl button and then press the W key twice (Ctrl+W+W). Then copy the four lines (go to the first line that you want to copy then type **4yy**). Use Ctrl+W+W to move forward until the cursor returns to the merged copy. Then move to where you want to make the change and press the P key.

After making all of your changes, you need to save and quit all four versions. The easiest way to do this is the `:wqa` vim command.

Merge all files and then stage/commit them with the `git commit -a` command.[8]

> **Git Humor**
>
> "Git knows what you did last summer!"
>
> —Anonymous

Summary

At this point you should now know how to create branches, see the difference in versions of files, and merge files from one branch to another.

---

8 If you are following along, be aware that at the end of this chapter I completed the merge of all files (including the `hidden.sh` file), committed all changes to the `test` branch, and pushed all changes for both the `test` and `master` branch to the central repository server.

Advanced Git Features

At the heart of Git are the repositories. Chapters 13 and 14 introduced you to tools that enabled you to work with the local repository. In this chapter you learn how to interact with the central repository server.

Managing Repositories

From your perspective, the central repository server is also considered the *remote* repository as opposed to the repository that is on your system (the *local* repository).

To see the location of your remote repository, execute the `git remote -v` command:

```
ocs@ubuntu:~/ocs$ git remote -v
origin  https://gitlab.com/borothwell/ocs.git (fetch)
origin  https://gitlab.com/borothwell/ocs.git (push)
```

Both lines point to the same location. The first line refers to the process of downloading content from the remote repository and the second line refers to the process of uploading content to the remote repository.

Very likely you will be working on separate projects, each with its own remote repository. To access another project, execute the `git remote add` command:[1]

```
ocs@ubuntu:~/ocs$ git remote add docs
➡ https://gitlab.com/borothwell/docs.git
ocs@ubuntu:~/ocs$ git remote -v
docs    https://gitlab.com/borothwell/docs.git (fetch)
docs    https://gitlab.com/borothwell/docs.git (push)
origin  https://gitlab.com/borothwell/ocs.git (fetch)
origin  https://gitlab.com/borothwell/ocs.git (push)
```

The `docs` argument is how you want to refer to this remote repository locally. The last argument is the URL path to the remote repository.

---

1 I created this new project by using the web interface provided by gitlab.com.

Of course, after you have added the remote repository, you should also clone it using the `git clone` command:

```
ocs@ubuntu:~/ocs$ cd ..
ocs@ubuntu:~$ git clone https://gitlab.com/borothwell/docs.git
Cloning into 'docs'...
Username for 'https://gitlab.com': borothwell
Password for 'https://borothwell@gitlab.com':
warning: You appear to have cloned an empty repository.
Checking connectivity... done.
ocs@ubuntu:~$ ls
docs  ocs
ocs@ubuntu:~$ ls -a docs
. .. .git
```

Even though this is an empty repository, you can see that it has been cloned by the fact it created a `~/docs` directory and a `docs/.git` directory. To perform work in this project, simply create files in the `~/docs` directory and execute the git commands while in this directory.

Getting Content from the Remote Server

The process of getting the content from the remote server to the local repository and working directory is fairly simple. In this situation, you execute the git clone command to duplicate everything in the project from the remote server to the local system.

However, this process can become much more complex later in the development cycle when you want to include changes from the remote server (likely from other developers) to your local repository and working directory. You can use several different methods, each with a different intended result.

Before getting into the process of getting content from the remote server, visualizing how content is sent from the working directory to other locations might be helpful. Look at Figure 15.1 for a demonstration.

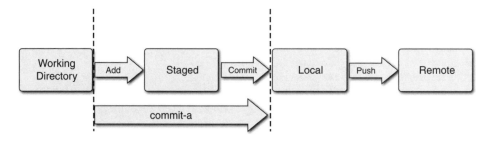

Figure 15.1   Git commands to send changes from the working directory

In Figure 15.1 you can see the flow of version changes. The `git add` command sends the working version to the staged area. The `git commit` command sends the staged version to the local repository. The `git commit -a` command can send a version from the working directory to the staged area and then to the local repository. Lastly, the git push command sends the changed versions of the files to the remote repository.[2]

When to Commit versus When to Push

I am often asked when to use `git commit` versus `git push`. Some organizations provide rules or guidelines for when a developer should use commit versus push. If your organization doesn't have any guidelines, I suggest using the following guidelines

- Commit often! It is the means by which you can undo a mistake or go back to an older version. Think of it like a "save as" of a document.
- Push when you have something to share to other developers. Pushing multiple times a day for subtle file changes makes the process of merging and applying changes much more difficult.

File versions cannot only be sent from the working directory up to the remote repository, but they can also be propagated from the remote repository to the local repository and the working directory. See Figure 15.2 for a visual description of the commands that can perform these actions.[3]

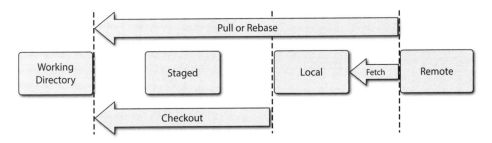

Figure 15.2   Git commands to retrieve changes from the remote repository

Details regarding these commands:

- The `git fetch` command downloads the latest version history of files from the remote repository to the local repository. This command does not change your working directory, but you can use the `git checkout` command to make the working directory contain the latest versions of the files of the branch.

---

2 None of these commands are new because they were covered in previous chapters. However, visualizing this process can help you understand the next topic better.

3 Note that the `git clone` command is not included in Figure 15.2. This is because typically you only run this command once when you first download the remote repository.

> **Important**
>
> The `git fetch` command only downloads the file versions. It does not perform any merging.
>
> - The `git pull` command downloads the latest version history of files from the remote repository to the local repository, but this command also performs a merge operation and updates the content of your working directory. The merging process is the same as that described in Chapter 14.
>
> - The `git rebase` command takes all the changes from a branch and applies them to the current branch. This is a process called *patching*, which is described in more detail later in this chapter.

Connecting via SSH

The default (and recommended) method of communication with the remote repository is HTTPS. Another method that can be used is SSH. Both methods should provide a secure (and encrypted) communication method. Typically, HTTPS is recommended for a few reasons:

- No additional setup is required when you use HTTPS. If you choose to use SSH, then you must generate a SSH key and upload it to the remote repository.

- When using HTTPS, Git makes use of a feature called **credential helper** automatically to cache your password. This means when you connect to the remote repository, you won't have to provide your password each time. This could also be configured for SSH, but it isn't done so automatically (you need to configure this using a SSH feature called **ssh-agent**).

- The third possible reason is related to firewalls. In networks that are highly secured with strict firewalls, the HTTPS network port is more likely to be "open" than the SSH network port.

This doesn't mean you shouldn't use SSH, just that the developers of Git recommend HTTPS. If you do want to use SSH, then you first need to execute the following command:

```
ocs@ubuntu:~/ocs$ ssh-keygen -t rsa
```

This creates an SSH key in the `~/.ssh/id_rsa.pub` file. You must upload this file to the SSH server, which you normally do via the web interface. See Figure 15.3 for an example of this interface on gitlab.com.

Figure 15.3   Uploading SSH keys on gitlab.com

After uploading the SSH keys to the remote repository server, you can have the `git` command use SSH instead of HTTP by using the following syntax:

```
git clone ssh://user@server/project.git
```

Another method that is popular is to use the following syntax:

```
git clone user@server:project.git
```

Patching

The idea of patching is that you will discover situations in which it won't be easy to perform a simple merge between two different branches. Several reasons exist as to why this might be, including the following:

- When you want to implement changes from a branch that hasn't been made available on the central repository

- When you want to implement changes from a specific version of a file

Actually several different techniques can be utilized to perform patching. The most basic (and common) method is to use the `git diff` command that was discussed in Chapter 14 to generate a diff file. You do this by executing the `git diff` command and redirecting the output to a file. For example:

```
git diff A B > file.patch
```

This patch file will be used to modify an existing checked-out file to include the differences. This is performed by using the `git apply` command. For example:

```
git apply file.patch
```

Often the patch file is generated on one system and then copied to another system before applying. It is also typically a good idea to use the `--check` option to test the patch before actually applying it:

```
git apply --check file.patch
git apply file.patch
```

> **Git Humor**
>
> "Nurture your git-twigs and they will grow into a full branch."
>
> —Anonymous

Summary

In this chapter you learned how to manage repositories. You also learned how to change the method of connecting to a remote repository from HTTPS to SSH. Last, you were introduced to the concept of patching in Git.

Index

REGISTER YOUR PRODUCT at informit.com/register
Access Additional Benefits and SAVE 35% on Your Next Purchase

- Download available product updates.

- Access bonus material when applicable.

- Receive exclusive offers on new editions and related products.
  (Just check the box to hear from us when setting up your account.)

- Get a coupon for 35% for your next purchase, valid for 30 days. Your code will
  be available in your InformIT cart. (You will also find it in the Manage Codes
  section of your account page.)

Registration benefits vary by product. Benefits will be listed on your account page
under Registered Products.

InformIT.com–The Trusted Technology Learning Source

InformIT is the online home of information technology brands at Pearson, the world's foremost
education company. At InformIT.com you can

- Shop our books, eBooks, software, and video training.
- Take advantage of our special offers and promotions (informit.com/promotions).
- Sign up for special offers and content newsletters (informit.com/newsletters).
- Read free articles and blogs by information technology experts.
- Access thousands of free chapters and video lessons.

Connect with InformIT–Visit informit.com/community

Learn about InformIT community events and programs.

informIT.com
the trusted technology learning source

Addison-Wesley · Cisco Press · IBM Press · Microsoft Press · Pearson IT Certification · Prentice Hall · Que · Sams · VMware Press

ALWAYS LEARNING   PEARSON